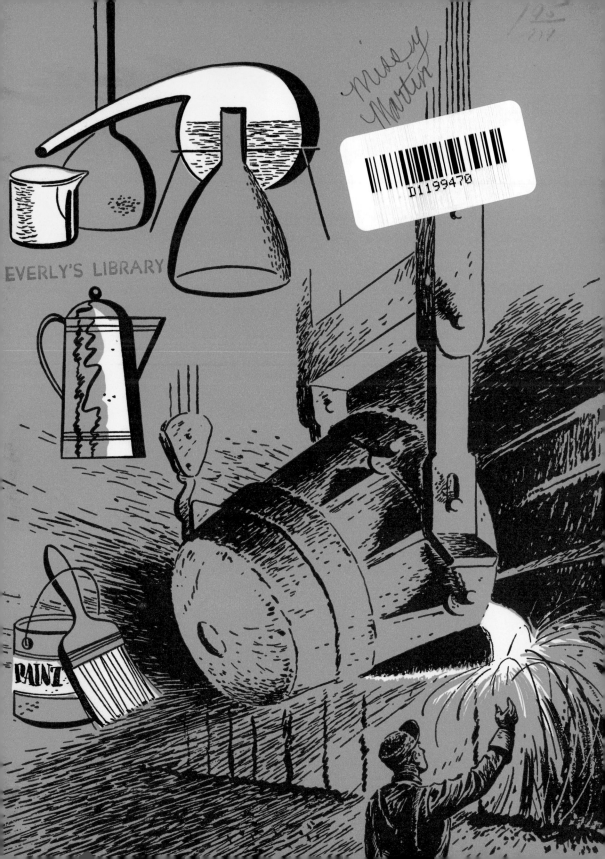

EVERLY'S LIBRARY

# All About
# the Wonders of
# Chemistry

By Ira M. Freeman

*Illustrated by George Wilde*

RANDOM HOUSE
NEW YORK

FOURTH PRINTING

COPYRIGHT 1954 BY IRA M. FREEMAN

LIBRARY OF CONGRESS CATALOG CARD NUMBER: 54-7002

MANUFACTURED IN THE U.S.A.

# Contents

The author wishes to thank the following
organizations for information which
was useful in the writing of this book:

*Copper & Brass Research Association*
*E. I. Du Pont de Nemours & Company*
*Esso Standard Oil Co.*
*The Firestone Tire & Rubber Company*
*Eli Lilly and Co.*
*Merck & Co., Inc.*
*Reynolds Metals Company*
*United States Steel Corporation*

# 1.

# How Chemistry Began

You are reading this book made of paper while sitting in a chair made of wood, in the light coming through a glass window. Often you ride along a concrete highway in an automobile constructed mostly of steel and powered by gasoline. Your food comes packed in glass, metal, paper or plastic containers. Hundreds of different materials are part of your way of living.

Select almost any object, and you will find that usually it can be formed from a choice of different materials. For instance, a drinking tumbler can be made of glass, porcelain, aluminum or plastic. And it is just as true that any chosen material can be formed into many different articles. For instance, from glass we can make a drinking tumbler, window pane, camera lens or lamp bulb.

A block of wood can be carved into the shape of a doll or a boat; yet we see that it is still a piece of wood. A teaspoonful of sugar seems to disappear when you dissolve it in water; yet you know it is still there by the sweet taste it gives to the water and you can get the sugar crystals back again by letting the water evaporate away.

We can change the shapes and forms of things easily, but to change the materials of which the things are made, we must turn to chemistry. Any change in the material itself, not just its form, is called a *chemical change*.

Chemical changes are constantly going on all around us. Iron rusts, milk turns sour, dead leaves decay. We cook food, wash clothes, drive cars, develop snapshots, light fires, varnish floors—all with the help of chemistry. Just the fact that you are alive means that some very complicated chemical changes are going on in your body all the time.

**Water may be in the form of a liquid, a solid or a gas.**

A single material can appear in different forms without going through a chemical change. Water running from the kitchen faucet looks quite different from the ice and snow we find outdoors on a cold day, but they are water, too—water in its solid form. Rising from the spout of a teakettle is a cloud of steam, which is water in the form of a gas. Just by changing the temperature we can have water in its three different forms—*solid, liquid* or *gas.*

Other materials, too, can take all three of these forms. Iron is usually a solid, but in a foundry it becomes a liquid and in the sun it exists as a gas. No matter what form it happens to be in, iron is still iron.

But there are also changes of a different kind going

on around us. If you burn a piece of wood, only a few bits of crumbling black charcoal are left. If you heat sugar in a spoon over a flame, you get a sticky brown mass of caramel. No amount of trying will change the charcoal back to wood or the caramel back to white sugar. It is as hopeless as trying to unscramble an egg! And this is because you have changed not only the form of the material; you have also changed it chemically.

The chemist is a scientist who studies chemical changes. He tries to find ways of turning familiar materials into new and different ones that will be even more useful to us.

Life was very different a hundred years ago, and many of the changes have been brought about by chemistry. Chemists have made our houses more comfortable, our clothing more efficient and our food more wholesome. Without modern chemistry we could have no trains, cars or airplanes to speed us from place to place. There would be no motion pictures, radio or television. Worst of all, we would not have the marvelous new medicines which now protect us against so many terrible diseases. Without the wonders of chemistry we would be little better off than the cave men who lived thousands of years ago.

The cave man who discovered fire was an early chemist.

The first chemist, in fact, was probably the unknown cave man who discovered how to make a fire. In the beginning he used it only for cooking his food. Later he discovered that when certain rocks were heated, shining metals would mysteriously appear. Somehow, in a hidden form, these metals must have been in the rocks in the first place. But it was a long time before people really understood what goes on when chemical changes take place. In early times they thought it was some kind of magic and asked no further questions.

Gradually, as civilization went forward, people began to wonder about their surroundings. They realized that certain materials were more common and more important than others. Besides fire, there was the water of the sea and of the rain. Underneath everything was the broad earth, and all around was the air which could not be seen but could be felt when the winds blew.

Later on, the famous Greek philosopher Aristotle took up this idea of earth, air, fire and water, and tried

The alchemists tried to change iron and lead into gold.

to explain how all things might be made up of mixtures of these four *elements*, as they were called. But Aristotle and his followers did not believe in doing any experiments to test their ideas. They did nothing more than talk about them and so did not get very far.

Meanwhile other people began to take an interest in the materials around them. One group called *alchemists* tried to find a way to change common metals like iron and lead directly into gold. They usually worked secretly over their experiments, boiling up all kinds of strange mixtures as they tried to discover the great trick that would make them rich and powerful.

For hundreds of years this working and testing went on. The alchemists believed there was some magic material called the Philosopher's Stone that was needed to turn things to gold. But try as they might, no such wonderful substance was ever found and not an ounce of gold was ever made. Sometimes an alchemist, in order to please a nobleman or a king, would secretly slip a piece of real gold into the mess he was cooking. Of course, if he was discovered doing this, his life was in danger.

At about the time Columbus sailed to America the alchemists began to have great doubts about ever being able to make gold, and they turned to making medicines. They still puttered about searching for the Philosopher's Stone because now they thought it would bring them the secret of everlasting health. So they worked on, stewing up all sorts of queer combinations. One of their favorite remedies was a mixture of gold, powdered lion's heart, witch hazel, earthworms and onions! Once in a while they happened to discover something that really worked, but more often their patients died because the drug proved to be a powerful poison instead of a cure.

We may laugh at the alchemists and drug-makers for their silly beliefs, but modern chemists owe them a great deal. At least they had curiosity about the nature of the world around them, and they were able to make other people take an interest in these questions too. Besides, they discovered some new metals and found out how to purify and separate mixed liquids by a method which is the same one used in modern chemical factories.

A liquid is usually a mixture of several things. In order to separate the different parts, chemists heat the liquid and each part boils off at a different temperature. At each step, the steam is led to another container which is then cooled, making the vapor turn to liquid again. This is called *distillation*. Later in this book you will see

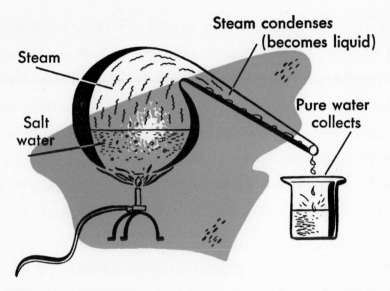

Steam

Steam condenses
(becomes liquid)

Salt
water

Pure water
collects

The salt remains while pure water condenses from the steam.

how petroleum is distilled in a refinery to become gasoline, lubricating oil and several other things.

The curious fact is that the secrets the alchemists searched for without success have really been discovered in the last few years. Naturally, our scientists of today did not get these results by finding some mysterious Philosopher's Stone or by muttering magic words over their experiments. Instead they used the method that all modern scientists use, carrying out carefully planned experiments and building up their knowledge bit by bit to get a sensible understanding of how Nature works.

Yes, science can actually change other materials into gold, but the process is so complicated that it does not pay. It is much easier and cheaper to dig gold out of the ground.

Chemists have turned their attention, instead, to the other dream of the alchemists—the search for the secrets of long life. And while no chemist has discovered a drug that will make people live forever, we now have wonderful remedies for many diseases that used to cripple and kill thousands of people. As you read this book, you will find out about some of these health-giving chemicals, as well as many others that help make our lives more comfortable, more interesting and safer. Compared with such treasures, gold is not very important after all.

# 2.

# What Our World Is Made of

Modern chemistry began at about the time our country got its independence. The question that interested scientists was an old one: "What happens when things burn?"

Up to that time, the best idea was that anything that could burn contained something they called *phlogiston*, (*flow-JISS-ton*) and that as the material burned, the phlogiston was given up. This seemed to be a sensible idea because after a piece of wood or coal is burned there is only a little ash left and most of the material itself has disappeared. So you can see why they dreamed up this mysterious, invisible phlogiston to explain what happens.

One of the people who wondered about the phlogiston idea was an English minister and amateur chemist named Joseph Priestley. He found that when a certain mineral was heated, a gas was given off. After filling a bottle with this gas, now called *oxygen*, he found that things burned more quickly in it than in open air. Then, over in France, a brilliant scientist named Antoine Lavoisier checked Priestley's experiment and went on to try something else. He heated a piece of tin in a bottle full of the new gas. The shiny metal surface became dull, and when the tin was weighed afterward it was found to be just a little heavier than before.

Lavoisier was puzzled and thought, "If phlogiston is given off, this piece of tin should weigh *less* than before." Actually, since it was heavier, it must have *taken on* something from the gas around it. Soon it was realized that the phlogiston idea had to be given up. We now know the real explanation. *When anything burns, the material joins up chemically with oxygen.*

It has always been known that, somehow, air is

needed when things burn, and the discovery of oxygen explained why. You can test this by standing a lighted candle in a dish of water and then covering the candle with a milk bottle. You find that the flame soon goes out. In the early days, chemists would have said that the air inside the bottle became so soaked with phlogiston from the burning candle that it put out the flame.

But you find, when the experiment is over, that the water has gone up part way inside the bottle. This must mean that something has been *taken out* of the air rather than *given to* it. About one-fifth of the air in the bottle is used up, so this much was oxygen. Almost all the rest of the air is another gas, called *nitrogen* (*NI-troh-jen*), which has nothing to do with burning. It has many other uses which you will read about later.

Most important of all, oxygen is used by all animals that breathe, including humans. Breathing is connected with a slow kind of burning. The food you eat is the fuel, and the heat created keeps your body at the proper temperature.

You remember that even as much as two thousand years ago the ancient Greeks tried to explain how all things are made up of the four elements earth, air, fire and water. When scientists began to experiment and find out more about materials, they realized that this idea was a good one, but that many more elements than four would be needed to explain the many different substances that were becoming known. They found several ways of breaking down materials in order to find out what is in them. Heating is one way. Passing a current of electricity through a liquid is another.

Suppose we want to find out what sugar is made of. We warm a spoonful of ordinary sugar over a flame and notice a crackling noise. At the same time, if we hold a knife blade over the sugar, a fog forms on it. The crackling sound and the appearance of moisture on the knife show that water has come from the sugar. As we con-

**By heating sugar, we find what it is made of.**

tinue to heat the sugar, it melts and darkens in color and finally becomes black as coal. It is, in fact, just that. Both coal and the black mass are *carbon*, which cannot be broken down into anything simpler.

But the water that came out of the sugar *can* be broken down further. When an electric current from a battery is sent through water containing some acid bubbles of oxygen come off one wire and bubbles of hydrogen appear at the other. These and about ninety other substances are called chemical *elements*. All other materials are made up of chemical

15

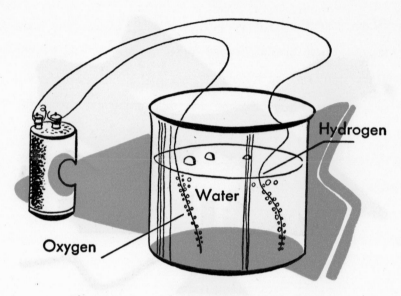

Electricity breaks up water into its elements.

combinations of the elements, and these combinations are called chemical *compounds*.

It took many years of patient work by scientists all over the world to discover the elements that we know. Silver, gold, tin and carbon were known from ancient times; but their importance as chemical elements was not understood. Other elements have been discovered in the last few years, and very likely still others will turn up in the future.

Most of the nearly one hundred elements are rare, and usually are not found in the common things around us. Nature seems to have added just a "pinch" of most of them when the universe was made. Actually, the ordinary materials of the earth, sea and air are made up of only about thirty elements. Here is a list of these elements. Alongside each name is the chemist's shorthand sign, or *symbol*, for each. Notice that some are solids, some are liquids and some are gases.

### SOME OF THE MORE PLENTIFUL CHEMICAL ELEMENTS

| Name | Symbol | Description |
| --- | --- | --- |
| Aluminum | Al | Lightweight silvery metal |
| Barium | Ba | Soft shiny metal |
| Bromine | Br | Heavy brown liquid |
| Calcium | Ca | Lightweight shiny metal |
| Carbon | C | Black solid, or clear crystals (diamond) |
| Chlorine | Cl | Greenish-yellow gas |
| Cobalt | Co | Crumbly gray metal |
| Copper | Cu | Soft reddish metal |
| Fluorine | F | Light yellow gas |
| Gold | Au | Heavy, soft, yellow metal |
| Hydrogen | H | Lightweight invisible gas |
| Iodine | I | Dark purple crystals |

## All About the Wonders of Chemistry

| Name | Symbol | Description |
| --- | --- | --- |
| Iron | Fe | Gray metal |
| Lead | Pb | Heavy, soft, blue-gray metal |
| Lithium | Li | Lightweight, soft, white metal |
| Magnesium | Mg | Lightweight white metal |
| Manganese | Mn | Crumbly, gray-white metal |
| Mercury | Hg | Heavy, silvery, liquid metal |
| Nickel | Ni | Hard white metal |
| Nitrogen | N | Invisible gas |
| Oxygen | O | Invisible gas |
| Phosphorus | P | Waxlike white solid |
| Potassium | K | Lightweight, soft, silvery metal |
| Silicon | Si | Crumbly gray crystals |
| Silver | Ag | Heavy, shiny white metal |
| Sodium | Na | Lightweight, soft, silvery metal |
| Sulfur | S | Light yellow, crumbly crystals |
| Tin | Sn | Silvery white metal |
| Titanium | Ti | Shiny white metal |
| Zinc | Zn | Crumbly, blue-white metal |

The chances are that you have never seen a great many of these elements. That is because they are usually locked up in compounds where they lose their identity. For example, sodium is a shiny metal and chlorine is a

**Lavoisier measured the exact weights of his chemicals.**

gas with an irritating smell, yet you sprinkle a compound of them on your food every day. Chemists call this compound *sodium chloride*. The common name is table salt. You would never guess that the white salt crystals have the metal and the greenish gas mysteriously locked up in them.

Sugar is a compound of carbon, oxygen and hydrogen. Although baking soda is a compound that contains exactly the same three elements as sugar, it has sodium besides and so it is quite different from sugar. Your own body contains thirteen well-known elements in many different combinations.

We know some of the elements in several different

physical forms. Carbon, for instance, has three forms. One is the crumbly, black material left over when sugar is charred or the toast is burned. Coal is mostly this form

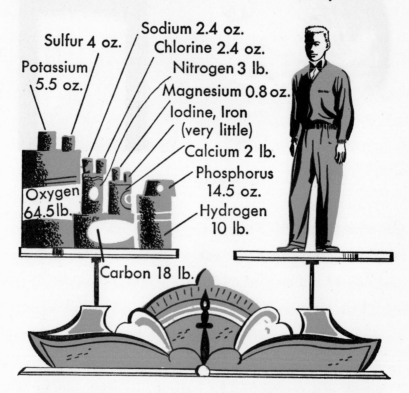

You are made of only a few cents' worth of chemicals.

of carbon. Another form of carbon is called *graphite*. This, too, is black, but is slippery and waxlike. Mixed with clay and molded into long, thin sticks it is the "lead" in a pencil. (The real element lead, Pb, is not used for this purpose.) The third form of carbon is very noble in appearance compared with its dark, smudgy brothers. It is in the shape of the beautiful, sparkling crystals we call *diamonds*. Chemically, any of the three forms of carbon is as good as another. Some rich man, if he were foolish enough, could burn diamonds in his furnace instead of coal. Diamonds are worth so much money only because they are rare.

Chemists today know of more than half a million different compounds, all formed from less than a hundred elements. This is possible because we can arrange a small number of things in many different *combinations*, just as we make many thousands of words out of the twenty-six letters of our alphabet.

As an example, take just the four letters, a, b, d and e. Out of only these four we can make the words

a     bad     be     bed

abed     bade     bead     dab

and if we allow ourselves to use the letters more than once, we can also make

add     bee     ebb     deed.

You can see that with twenty-six letters, using them as often as we please, we can get the large number of words the English language contains.

But our language does not use *all* the combinations

you might get by throwing together letters. Such groups as *adeb*, *beda*, and *deab* can be made from a, b, d and e, but these are not real words. The same thing is true for chemical combinations. You could think up groups such

as ClO or HCNa or millions of others, but no such compounds ever form. True, you can *mix* any elements you please, but only in certain cases will they actually hook up into chemical compounds. Just how this works out is explained in the next chapter.

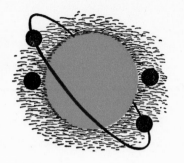

# 3.

# The Chemist Builds Molecules

The word "atom" is one that we hear very often these days. We read about "atomic energy," "atom bombs" and "atomic power" and perhaps get the idea that atoms are something new. Far from it! People were thinking about atoms over 2,000 years ago, but this idea did not come to mean much in chemistry until about 150 years ago. This was the time of the great Napoleon. Most people do not know that it was also the time when John Dalton, a modest schoolteacher in England, put the atom idea into chemistry. This turned out to be much more important to the world than any battles Napoleon fought.

Back in ancient times, people wondered about an interesting problem: Suppose you take a piece of some material and break it in two. Then take one of these pieces and break it in two, and continue to do this. Is there any limit to how far you can go? Some people believed that this chopping up could be carried on without ever ending. Others thought that it could be done only until you got down to a single *atom*, the smallest particle of the material that can exist. They had the feeling that every material was made up of very tiny particles, so small that they could not be seen.

In those days the atom idea was just a "hunch." Much later, scientists were able to show that atoms really did exist, and that with this idea many things could be explained. It turned out that atoms are even smaller than the ancients dreamed. They are far too tiny to be seen even with the strongest microscopes. If a single drop of water could be enlarged to the size of the earth, the atoms in it would be only about as big as basketballs. There are about three million billion carbon atoms in the ink in the period at the end of this sentence.

Since nobody has ever seen a single atom directly, how

**How far can this chopping up be carried on?**

do we know that there are such things? The answer is that scientists have discovered many facts which can be explained only if we *take for granted* that there are such atoms. This is just as reliable as actually seeing the atoms. Do not doubt this kind of explanation, because we use it all the time in many familiar cases. For example, suppose you see a hunter raise a gun to his shoulder and aim at a squirrel. Then you hear a loud BANG and see the squirrel drop dead in his tracks. You would naturally *take it for granted* that a bullet killed the animal, although you did not actually see the bullet in flight. You would not even listen to any other explanation.

That is how it is with our knowledge of atoms. It is an idea that works, and atoms are just as real to a scientist as marbles and baseballs are to you. Not only does he believe in atoms, but he has been able to count them, to weigh them and to find out how big they are—all without ever having seen one.

Now let us see what all this talk of atoms has to do with chemistry. Chemist John Dalton decided to find out *how much* of each element is needed to form its compounds. He experimented with many combinations and found that he could always *mix* a couple of elements in any amounts he pleased, but if he wanted to form an actual *compound* of the two, they had to be used only in a certain proportion. If not, some of one or the other would be left over. Nature seems to be very particular about the amounts of materials that can be joined chemically.

Dalton reasoned that this was because the elements are made up of atoms. He said to himself, "Suppose all the atoms of one element are alike, but different from the atoms of any other element. Also, suppose that whenever two elements form a compound, a definite number of atoms of the first element always join up with a definite number of the other. Why, there we have it! That explains why the needed amount of the two elements never changes."

For example, here is how it works out for water,

which is a compound of oxygen and hydrogen. Whenever chemists want to combine these two elements to form water, they find they must use them in a certain *proportion*, which is always the same, no matter whether they are forming a single drop of water or many gallons. By measuring the proportion of hydrogen and oxygen needed, they find that each atom of oxygen must grab up and hold on to *two* atoms of hydrogen. This is the meaning of the familiar sign "$H_2O$" for water.

**Three atoms join up to form a molecule of water ($H_2O$).**

Now everything begins to fall into place. A definite hook-up of atoms is called a *molecule*, and every compound is a collection of molecules that are all alike. Each of these molecules can contain only a definite number of atoms of each of its elements. It is very much like forming a baseball team. You must use one pitcher, one catcher, one shortstop, three basemen and three fielders. No other combination will produce a regulation ball team. Any additional players must only remain on the sidelines.

The chemical sign, or *formula*, for a molecule of common salt is NaCl, which means that each molecule of salt is a combination of one atom of sodium (Na) and one atom of chlorine (Cl). The chemical name for table salt is *sodium chloride*, and to tell someone the formula for it you would just say the four letters "N-A-C-L." Iron rust is *ferric oxide*, $Fe_2O_3$; so each molecule of this compound is made up of two iron atoms (Fe) joined with three oxygen atoms (O). In speaking of it you would say, "F-E-2-O-3."

That is the way it goes for hundreds of thousands of other compounds. Later on you will meet some complicated molecules that have half a dozen different kinds of atoms in them. The chemist is a builder of molecules, and he uses atoms of the elements as his "bricks."

Here is a list of a few familiar compounds, giving the chemical name and formula of each one:

| *Common Name* | *Chemical Name* | *Formula* |
|---|---|---|
| Baking soda | sodium bicarbonate | $Na\,H\,CO_3$ |
| Cane sugar | sucrose | $C_{12}H_{22}O_{11}$ |
| Cleaning fluid | carbon tetrachloride | $CCl_4$ |
| Grain alcohol | ethanol | $C_2H_6O$ |
| Household ammonia | ammonium hydroxide | $NH_5O$ |
| Laundry starch | starch | $C_6H_{10}O_5$ |
| Limestone | calcium carbonate | $CaCO_3$ |
| Moth flakes | naphthalene | $C_{10}H_8$ |
| Vinegar | acetic acid | $C_2H_4O_2$ |
| Washing soda | sodium carbonate | $Na_2CO_3$ |

Notice that such different compounds as sugar, alcohol, starch and vinegar are all made of the very same elements. These compounds are quite distinct from each

other only because their molecules have *different numbers* of atoms in them.

Most of the familiar materials around us are mixtures of compounds. Milk, wood, orange juice, paper, gasoline and steel are all mixtures of this kind. Sea water is a mixture of several compounds all dissolved in the water. Soil is a mixture of a great many compounds. Air happens to be a mixture made up almost entirely of *elements*, mostly oxygen and nitrogen. Brass is also a mixture of elements, mainly copper and zinc.

Do you remember, at the end of the last chapter, how molecules were compared with words, and atoms were like the letters that form the words? You found, too, that there were many combinations of letters that did not make regular words. In the same way, many groupings of atoms that a chemist might dream up never form at all because atoms can choose their partners only in certain ways. Each kind of atom seems to have a definite number of "hands" that it can use to hold on to other atoms. The number of hands is called the *valence* (*VAY-lence*) of the atom.

A hydrogen atom has a valence of 1, which means that it has only a single hand. An oxygen atom has a valence of 2, so it can grab and hold on to two hydro-

A neon atom says "Hands off" to all other atoms.

gens; forming a molecule of water, $H_2O$. Sodium and chlorine are each "one-handed" atoms. They can form sodium chloride, NaCl, in which one atom of sodium combines with one atom of chlorine. However, you can see that there can be no such compound as $NaCl_2$ because one of the chlorines would have nothing to hold on to. But $CaCl_2$ does exist because calcium has two hands and so can hold both chlorine atoms.

Both gold and silver have a valence of 1, calcium 2, aluminum 3. A very few elements, such as helium and neon, say "hands off" to all other atoms. They have the valence *zero*, and do not combine with anything. Most atoms, however, have their valence between 1 and 7. Some elements, especially carbon, have more than one valence number and this makes it possible to form many more compounds.

Of course the chemist does not believe that atoms are really little dwarfs that join hands with each other. Nowadays he knows that all atoms contain tiny bits of electricity, called *electrons*, and he can understand valence as the holding-together of atoms by the pulling effect of the electrons in them.

# 4.

# Oil—The Chemist's Treasure Chest

Except for water, petroleum is probably the most useful and valuable liquid on earth. Petroleum (crude oil) is found deep in the ground in many parts of the world. From it we get gasoline, kerosene, all sorts of lubricating oils, waxes, greases, and many other useful materials. Our modern cars, planes, railroad trains and other machines could not run without its products.

Although petroleum has been known for thousands of years, it was not until about the time of the Civil War that people found a way to drill deep into the earth to get petroleum out in large quantities. Up to that time, homes, stores and factories were lit by lamps that burned whale oil.

Soon oil wells were being drilled in many places and derricks became a familiar sight in Pennsylvania, Oklahoma, Texas and California. New towns sprang up wherever oil was found. Great oil fields were later discovered in Russia, Arabia, South America and the islands of the East Indies. Today the world produces nearly two billion barrels of petroleum each year, enough to form a lake one mile square and 300 feet deep. About two-thirds of this comes from the United States.

Finding the crude oil and getting it out of the ground is only the first step. Before this dark-colored, bad-smelling liquid mixture can be made to give up the many useful materials it contains, it must be *refined*. This is usually done by distillation, which is a process that was described on page 8. The petroleum is heated slowly in a large tank. At first, only the lightest liquids in the mixture boil off and the vapors are led off to another tank and cooled until they become a liquid again. These are chemicals like naphtha, which is used in making varnish.

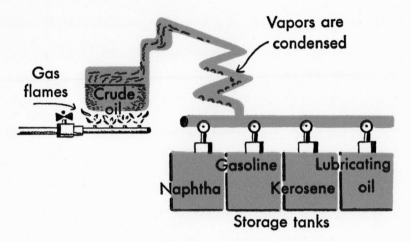

Petroleum (crude oil) is refined by distilling.

Next, the remaining crude oil is made a little hotter and the mixture we call gasoline comes off. Increasing the heat by further steps brings out kerosene, lubricating oils, greases, vaseline, paraffin and asphalt, one after another. These products may be further refined by distilling them again. Then they can be made into such useful things as paving materials, linoleum, insect sprays, paint, cold cream, candles, artificial rubber, and dozens more.

What kind of a chemical is petroleum and where did it come from? Scientists believe that millions of years ago, tiny plants and animals in the sea collected at the bottom when they died and were later covered over with sand. The sand finally became rock, and the decayed remains of these little creatures turned into a dark, oily liquid. Much later, when the rock became dry land, people discovered the oil in it.

The chemist finds that petroleum is a mixture of nearly sixty compounds, called *hydrocarbons*. Each molecule of such a compound is a chain of carbon atoms with hydrogen atoms hooked on. Carbon is a wonderful element, and the reason is that its atoms are chemically very chummy. They seem to like to form combinations, and they even combine with each other. Carbon usually has a valence of 4. Remember, this means that each carbon atom can be imagined to have four "hands" for holding on to other atoms (page 30). For instance, one carbon atom can grab four hydrogen atoms to form a molecule of methane (*METH-ayn*), which is the simplest compound found in petroleum. We could picture a methane molecule like this:

The next compound in the set has two carbons and six hydrogens. It is called ethane (*ETH-ayn*) and looks like this:

From now on, we will draw our diagrams of molecules as the chemist does, using chemical symbols for the atoms and a short line to stand for each pair of clasped hands between two atoms. Chemists call such a link a *valence bond*. The picture formula of the molecule showing how its atoms are linked together is called its *structural formula*. Then, as chemists sketch them, methane and ethane look like this:

Methane          Ethane

And here are a few more of the compounds found in petroleum:

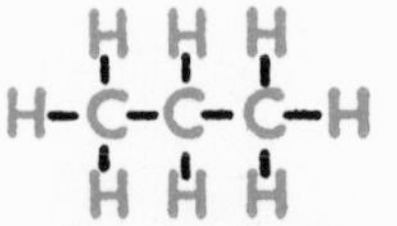

Propane

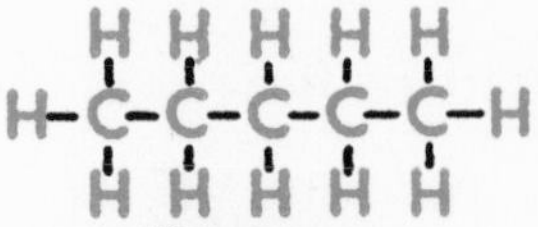

Pentane

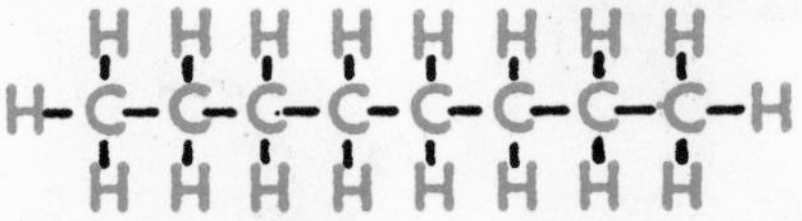

Octane

Notice how they are all built on the same chainlike pattern. The longest and heaviest hydrocarbon molecule in petroleum has sixty carbon atoms in its chain. Its formula is $C_{60}H_{122}$.

When crude oil is distilled, the light molecules containing about six to twelve carbon atoms are collected in one batch. After further distillation and chemical treatment, this mixture becomes what we call gasoline. In the carburetor of an automobile engine, the liquid gasoline is vaporized (changed to a gas) and mixed with air. The spark plugs make this mixture explode in the cylinders of the engine, and this furnishes the power to drive the car.

There are so many cars, trucks and airplanes now in use that not enough gasoline can be obtained for them just by distilling crude petroleum. Luckily, chemists have found ways of "making" molecules artificially for this purpose. One of the methods is called *cracking*. The fuel oil used to heat buildings and run Diesel trains and ships is a mixture of hydrocarbon molecules that are several times as long as the ones in gasoline. When this oil is put under pressure and at the same time strongly heated, the long chains break into shorter ones to form a good gasoline. In this way we can now get nearly twice as much gasoline from each barrel of crude oil.

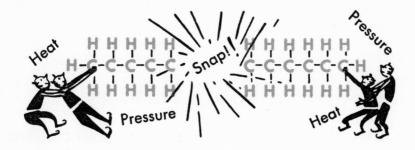

Another way to get even more gasoline from petroleum is to make some of its smaller chain molecules join into longer chains. Chemists have found how to do this, and they call such put-together molecules *polymers* (*POLLY-murz*). You may have seen advertisements mentioning "poly gas." In still another process, gasoline, fuel oil and cooking gas can be made from coal.

# 5.

# The Atoms Choose Partners

About nineteen out of every twenty known chemical compounds have carbon in them. Almost everything you eat or wear contains carbon compounds, and so do many hundreds of everyday materials such as dyes, medicines, plastics and soaps.

The thing that makes carbon such an unusually useful element is the sociability of carbon atoms. They like to get together with each other and with other kinds of atoms to form molecules. Some of these molecules are fairly simple and have only a few atoms in them, while others are much larger and are made up of many hundreds of atoms. Your own body contains some of the most complicated of all carbon compounds, and chemists are still trying to find out how these molecules are built up.

In the early days of chemistry, people thought that carbon compounds were formed by some mysterious "life force" believed to be found only in living things. They called all compounds of carbon *organic compounds*, meaning that they are formed only in living organisms (plants or animals).

But some scientists doubted the "life force" idea. Among them was a young German chemist named Wöhler. Starting with ordinary chemicals, he was able to form a carbon compound called *urea* (*you-REE-uh*) which, up to that time, was found only in the kidneys of animals. Although this discovery proved that organic compounds could be made in a laboratory without the help of any animal or plant, Wöhler did not tell anyone about his work for three years because he was afraid that people would not believe him.

As time went on, chemists worked out ways of putting together many other organic materials. Today, almost any compound found in living things can be produced in a laboratory by starting with minerals such as limestone and coal. But chemists still keep the name *organic chemistry* for the branch of their subject that has to do with carbon compounds. The study of all other compounds—the ones that do not contain carbon —is called *inorganic chemistry*.

From the last chapter you remember that petroleum is a mixture of many different hydrocarbon molecules with their carbon atoms arranged in long chains. One thing the chemist can do is to make the carbons join hands in a different way. Here, for example, is a molecule of a compound called normal butane (*BUE-tayn*):

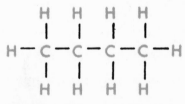

Normal butane (C$_4$H$_{10}$)

As in other chain hydrocarbons, each of the four valence bonds ("hands") of a carbon atom holds on to either another carbon atom or a hydrogen atom. The chemist can change the normal butane molecule to isobutane (*EYE-suh-BUE-tayn*), which looks like this:

```
        H   H   H
        |   |   |
    H — C — C — C — H
        |   |   |
        H   |   H
            |
        H — C — H
            |
            H
```

Isobutane ($C_4H_{10}$)

Here one carbon has been taken from the chain and stuck on to the middle carbon of the three that are left. Although both molecules are built of the same atoms, the difference in the way these atoms are connected means that the two are quite different substances. The ordinary formula is the same for both $C_4H_{10}$. The real difference is shown only when we draw a picture of the way the atoms are joined.

The change from butane to isobutane is just one example of how the atoms in a molecule can be re-arranged. With the longer chain molecules there are many more possible hookups. By the time we get to $C_{20}H_{42}$ there are more than 100,000 possibilities, but only a very few of these have actually been made. The different arrangements of a single molecule are called isomers (*EYE-suh-murz*).

As if this were not enough, carbon atoms are so anxious to hold on to other atoms that they sometimes use two and even three pairs of hands to do so! When coal or wood or hydrocarbons burn, each atom of carbon joins with the two atoms of oxygen to form a molecule of the gas known as carbon dioxide (*die-OCK-side*), $CO_2$. You know this invisible gas as the one that makes a soda fizz. It is also used to fill fire extinguishers and to make bread rise. "Dry ice" is carbon dioxide that has been frozen solid. The structural formula of carbon dioxide looks like this:

$$O = C = O$$

Notice the *double bond* between the carbon and each of the oxygens.

Some compounds have a double bond between two carbons. An example is ethylene (*eth-uh-LEAN*), a gas used for ripening fruit and as an anesthetic. Its molecule has this structure:

$$H- C = C - H$$

Ethylene

By making more carbons and more hydrogens attach themselves to the ethylene molecule, chemists can make these,

$$
\begin{array}{c}
\quad\; \overset{\displaystyle H}{|} \\
H-\overset{|}{\underset{|}{C}}-C=C-H \\
\;\; H \;\; H \;\; H
\end{array}
\qquad
\begin{array}{c}
\quad\; \overset{\displaystyle H}{|} \qquad\;\; \overset{\displaystyle H}{|} \\
H-\overset{|}{\underset{|}{C}}-C=C-\overset{|}{\underset{|}{C}}-H \\
\;\; H \;\; H \;\; H \;\; H
\end{array}
$$

Propylene      Butylene

and many other molecules. Some are formed in the "cracking" process for making gasoline. They burn more slowly than the regular chain molecules and so prevent the engine from "knocking."

In still another kind of hydrocarbon there is a *triple bond* between carbon atoms. Acetylene (*uh-SET-uh-lean*), a gas that burns with a very hot flame used for cutting and welding metals, has this structural formula:

$$H - C \equiv C - H$$

Acetylene

Another compound, used in making plastics and artificial rubber, has a single, a double and a triple bond between carbon atoms:

$$
\begin{array}{c}
\;\; \overset{\displaystyle H}{|} \\
C = C - C \equiv C \\
| \qquad | \qquad\qquad | \\
H \quad H \qquad\quad H
\end{array}
$$

Vinylacetylene

In spite of all these possibilities, there was one group of compounds that puzzled chemists for many years. The simplest one of this set is called benzene (*BEN-zean*) and its ordinary formula is $C_6H_6$. But nobody seemed to be able to figure out the structural formula of the molecule. No matter how he imagined the atoms to be hooked together, the pattern never seemed to come out right. The problem was finally solved by a dream! The dreamer was a chemist named Kekulé (*KAY-koo-lay*) who lived about a hundred years ago.

One day, while working in his laboratory in Belgium, he became tired and decided to rest for a while in his chair before the fireplace. As he watched the flickering flames, he became drowsy and must have fallen asleep. The flames seemed to become atoms that darted and danced before his eyes. They formed long rows that twisted and turned like snakes. All at once, one of the snakes grabbed his own tail in his mouth.

Kekulé suddenly woke up with a start. That was it! In great excitement, he dashed to his desk and began sketching chemical symbols. He worked far into the night until at last he had the answer: The benzene molecule was a *ring* of atoms—a chain whose ends were joined. Here is what he drew:

H
|
C
H C = C H
C C
C C
H C = C H
|
H

The picture fitted all the facts known about this molecule, and was named the *benzene ring*. It was the master plan for building new molecules of many kinds.

Chemists all over the world now use structural formulas as a guide for making many useful substances never known before. They really "design" new molecules in advance, just as an architect makes plans for a house before starting to build it. In working out these designs, organic chemists are not ashamed to play with building blocks. They actually use colored wooden or plastic balls to stand for the atoms, and fasten them together with short rods that fit into holes in the balls. In this way they can tell how to change a molecule, lopping off an atom and replacing it with some other kind of atom, or whole group of atoms, to make an entirely new material.

Here is the ball-and-rod model of a compound called

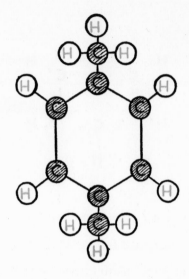

xylene (*Zl-lean*). It looks like some fancy kind of television antenna. When the chemist wanted to make this material, he said to himself, "Let's see if we can take off the hydrogens at the top and bottom of the benzene ring and stick on a $CH_3$ group in place of each one." He could even tell beforehand what this new compound would be like. Then he went into the laboratory and worked out a way of actually making it.

The planning, with the help of the model, had to come first. Otherwise, organic chemistry would be a hit-and-miss affair, and the chances are that many of the valuable compounds we use today in our homes, in factories, on farms and in hospitals would still be undiscovered.

# 6.

# The Chemist in the Steel Mill

If you have ever visited Pittsburgh, Gary, Cleveland or Birmingham, you may know what an active and busy place a huge steel mill is. Great blast furnaces, over a hundred feet tall, send clouds of smoke high into the air. Near by, giant cranes dip their buckets into the holds of ships to unload cargoes of iron ore. From inside of long, low buildings come deafening sounds as the white-hot steel is shaped into sheets, rails, pipes and beams. At night, flames and showers of sparks light up the sky for miles around.

## All About the Wonders of Chemistry

What goes on in such a smoky, noisy steel mill does not seem to have much to do with the work of a chemist, yet steel making is really a series of chemical changes, and modern steel mills have many chemists working for them. These scientists keep a constant check on the 120 million tons of steel that come from the mills each year. This would be enough to give each man, woman and child in the United States a 17-inch cube of steel weighing about three-quarters of a ton.

There is no question about the value of steel in modern life. It is our strongest material. Without it there would be no tall buildings, no large bridges, trains, ships,

Chemistry is very important in every steel mill.

cars or planes. There would be no machinery for farming and no cans in which to pack farm products. Nor would there be any printing presses, electric motors, telephones or tools.

Where does steel come from? Steel is a mixture of the element iron (Fe) with small amounts of carbon and other elements. Iron is not found in the ground as a metal but only in the form of *iron ore* which is usually a compound of iron and oxygen. Huge deposits of the reddish-brown ore are found in Minnesota, Alabama and several other states. After being dug out of the ground, the ore is sent to the mills where the metal is freed from its chemical partner, oxygen.

A compound of any metal with oxygen is called an *oxide* (*OCK-side*) of the metal. Iron ore is an *iron oxide*, not very different from ordinary iron rust. The action of breaking up the oxide to get the metal itself is called *smelting*. But the oxygen atoms hold the iron atoms very tightly, so the oxygen has to be coaxed away by giving it some carbon to combine with. This is done by putting coke into the blast furnace along with iron ore. Coke is made by distilling coal and is almost pure carbon.

Hot air is blown through the mixture to make the

coke burn (that is where the name *blast* furnace comes from). This burning produces not only heat but also *carbon monoxide*, the very poisonous gas that comes from the exhaust pipe of a car. In the blast furnace the carbon monoxide does the useful job of taking the oxygen away from the iron oxide, leaving iron metal which collects in drops and falls to the bottom of the furnace.

Iron ore often contains small amounts of other metals which must be removed when the ore is smelted. This is done by putting limestone into the blast furnace where it combines with the silicon and other impurities to form a waste material called *slag*.

Once a blast furnace is started, it is run without stopping for months or even years. More than a ton of ore, coke and limestone is dumped in each minute. In this same time, enough air to fill your whole house has been heated to a temperature of 1,000 degrees and blown through the mixture. Every six hours the white-hot liquid iron is allowed to flow out of the bottom of the furnace. It may be run into molds where it hardens in the shape of big blocks of "pig iron" or taken away in special cars while it stays liquid, to be made into steel. A large furnace can put out more than fifty tons of iron every hour.

**Iron oxide is broken up in a blast furnace.**

Each time a batch of melted iron is drawn off from the blast furnace, a sample is put aside to harden and is rushed to the chemical laboratory, where it is analyzed to find out what elements are mixed in with the iron. By using regular chemical methods it took many hours in the past to find out what a sample of iron contained.

First the iron had to be dissolved in acid; then various chemicals were added to form compounds with the elements in the sample. By recognizing these compounds, the chemist was able to tell what elements were present. All of this took many hours.

A chemist uses a spectrograph to analyze a sample of steel.

Nowadays the chemist takes a short cut by using an instrument called a *spectrograph*. He lets an electric current jump between two rods made of the iron sample. The dazzling light from this spark goes into the spectrograph, which sorts out the different colors in it. In a few minutes the chemist has a record of all these colors in the form of lines on a photographic film.

Each chemical element gives out only a certain set of lines, so that by looking at the picture, the chemist can tell exactly which elements were in the sample of iron. And from the brightness of the lines he can tell just about how much of each element it contained. This information is very important, because it tells him what to add or take away in order to make different kinds of steel from the iron.

As it comes from the blast furnace, iron usually has small amounts of carbon, manganese, silicon, phosphorus and sulfur in it. This is all right for making *cast iron* sinks, bathtubs, pipes and machine parts. But it is too brittle, too easily cracked and broken, for many other uses.

Scientists have found that it is mainly the carbon in blast-furnace iron that makes it brittle, so they burn out, or oxidize, most of the carbon in order to change the iron into *steel*. In one way of doing this, about twenty tons of the liquid iron is dumped into a large egg-shaped container called a Bessemer converter, named for the man who invented it about a hundred years ago. The converter is turned straight up and a blast of air is blown through the liquid iron. This burns out the carbon and also the silicon and manganese, sending up a giant flame nearly a hundred feet high and throwing out a dazzling shower of "sparklers." After about fifteen minutes, the flame dies down and the steel maker knows that the impurities have been burned out, changing the iron to steel. The converter is then tipped down again, the air blast is shut off and the steel is poured off into a huge "ladle."

For making steel of greater purity, an *open hearth* furnace is used. Several hundred tons of iron are poured into the "hearth," which is shaped like a huge dish. Limestone, scrap iron and iron ore are added. Then long flames from burning gas or oil are shot across the top of the liquid iron, raising the temperature to 3,000 degrees. This terrific heat burns out the impurities, and after about twelve hours the finished steel is allowed to run out into a ladle. Meanwhile, the phosphorus in the iron has combined with other materials and can be skimmed off the liquid steel in the form of a slag, to be used later in making fertilizer.

No matter whether the steel is made in a converter, in an open hearth or even in an electric furnace, chemists keep a careful check on its chemical make-up. Then, when it is taken out of the furnace, exact amounts of various materials are added to make it just right for its special use. The chemist acts like a cook, giving the steel maker a "recipe" for preparing different mixtures of

**Liquid iron is dumped into the Bessemer converter.**

steel with other metals. Such a mixture of metals is called an *alloy*.

For instance, a hard, tough steel is needed for making safes, machine tools and armor plate for battleships and tanks. The chemist will say, "Add 10 percent of manganese," or "Put in 6 percent of nickel." A maker of pots and pans or surgical instruments wants a *stainless steel*—one that does not tarnish when used in the kitchen or hospital. The steel man makes it by adding some chromium to the raw steel. Magnets used in electric motors are made of steel having some silicon in it. Adding a different amount of silicon makes steel that can be used for automobile springs. Elements such as wolfram, molybdenum and vanadium are used in making other special alloys. Usually only small amounts of these metals are needed to make great changes in the steel.

After it has been poured into molds, the steel hardens into big blocks called *ingots*. Next it goes through the rolling mill where the ingots are squeezed back and forth between gigantic rollers that flatten them out like dough, forming steel sheets, bars, rails or girders. A rod can be pulled through smaller and smaller holes until it becomes wire, or a bar can have a hole pushed through it to form a pipe. A disk of hot steel can be shaped into a railroad car wheel in a huge press that squeezes it with as much force as the weight of a battleship.

These and thousands of other steel products, from carpet tacks to locomotives, are here for our use because scientists have found out so much about the chemistry of this wonderful material.

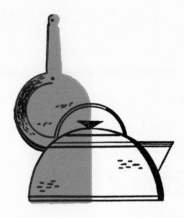

# 7.

# Some Other Useful Metals

Aluminum makes up about one-twelfth of the material of soil and rocks. Like iron, this element is always found combined with other elements, mostly oxygen, but it is much harder to get aluminum out of its compounds than to free iron from its ores. That is why, even though aluminum is one of the most common elements on earth, it was practically unknown until about a hundred years ago, while iron has been in use for thousands of years.

## All About the Wonders of Chemistry

When Napoleon gave a banquet, only the most honored guests were served with aluminum knives and forks. The less important ones had to use gold or silver! At that time, aluminum cost over $500 a pound. Now it sells for less than fourteen cents a pound, and more than half a million tons are used every year.

The cause of this great change was a discovery made about seventy years ago by a 23-year-old chemistry student named Charles Hall. One day Hall was listening to a chemistry lecture at Oberlin College in Ohio. The professor was talking about aluminum and said, "Any person who discovers a process by which aluminum can be made on a commercial scale will bless humanity and make a fortune for himself."

This made a great impression on young Hall, and he made up his mind to work on this problem. He borrowed some chemical equipment and set up a laboratory in a woodshed back of his house. Two years later he rushed excitedly into his professor's office and laid a few small lumps of silvery metal on the desk. It was aluminum! The search had been successful, and in a short time the Hall method for making aluminum was in general use. It is the method used today.

The starting point is an aluminum ore called bauxite

(*BAWK-site*), an oxide of the metal. Hall found that this oxide would dissolve in another compound of aluminum, called cryolite (*KRI-oh-lite*), when the cryolite was melted. Then he sent an electric current through the mixture, and liquid aluminum metal began to gather at the bottom of the tub. The picture shows

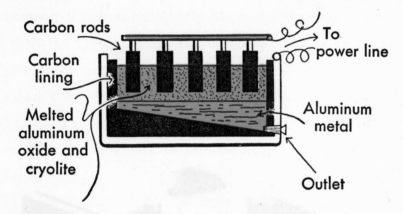

**Aluminum metal is separated from its ore by electricity.**

the arrangement used in an aluminum plant. The process is called *electrolysis*. Oxygen set free by the current combines with the carbon of the rods to form carbon dioxide. The melted aluminum can be drained off into molds and allowed to harden. There may be several hundred of these tubs in a factory, and together they use as much electric current as a large city.

Aluminum is particularly useful because of its lightness. It is only about one-third as heavy as steel, yet it can be made nearly as strong by alloying it with other metals such as copper and magnesium. Because of their lightness, aluminum alloys are used in many parts of airplanes, cars, buses, railroad trains and even the walls of buildings.

Another good feature of aluminum is that it protects itself against the weather by forming a layer of oxide. This layer is only a few millionths of an inch thick, but it sticks to the metal like a skin. On the other hand, when iron rusts, the oxide crumbles off and soon the

In this plant you see a long row of aluminum-producing cells.

whole piece is rusted away.

It would be impossible to mention all the many uses of aluminum. It is being used more and more instead of copper for cross-country electric power lines. It is an ideal metal for making pots and pans, vacuum cleaners, toasters and many parts of refrigerators. The aluminum foil that is used to wrap chewing gum is only about one-sixteenth as thick as a page of this book. Slightly heavier foil is used as an airtight wrapping for candy bars, cigarettes and all kinds of food products. Tiny flakes of the metal are used in making aluminum paint. In place of silver, astronomers now use a coating of pure aluminum on the mirrors of their telescopes. Every year new uses are being found for this exceptional metal, and in many cases it will eventually replace steel.

More than three-quarters of all the elements are metals.

Along with aluminum, copper is one of the most interesting and useful. It was one of the first metals people knew about, probably because it is found as lumps of metal, not combined with other elements. Many thousand years ago the Egyptians found they could shape this reddish metal into spears, hatchets, tools and ornaments. It was much easier to hammer the soft copper than to chip forms out of stone. They also made many things of *bronze* by alloying copper with tin and zinc. Later they found out how to make *brass*, an alloy of copper and zinc alone.

Although copper can sometimes be found in the ground as lumps of metal, most of it is in the form of ores in which it is combined with sulfur or oxygen. After it is dug out of the ground, the ore is crushed and washed. Then it goes to the smelter, where it is made to combine with oxygen in order to get rid of all the sulfur. Then the metal is freed from oxygen by putting the oxide into a blast furnace. Finally, it goes to a converter where air is blown through it to take out some of the impurities, very much like the method used for making steel.

About half of all the copper produced is used in the electrical industry, because electric currents can pass

The ore lies near the surface in an open-pit copper mine.

through a copper wire more easily than through any other common metal. But the copper must be very pure for this use; so it goes through an electrolysis process very much like the one used to get aluminum. The result is copper that is 99.95 percent pure. The impurities which fall to the bottom of the tank are valuable too. They contain silver and gold, which can be recovered.

Besides its use for making electric wires and cables, copper serves many other purposes. In your home, you may have copper screens and cooking pots. Copper tubing is used to make boilers, and heating and water pipes. An automobile contains about forty-five pounds of copper. Millions of pounds of this metal are used in building a large ship.

When exposed to air, copper forms a protective skin, just as aluminum does. Moisture and carbon dioxide in the air combine with the copper to make a protective greenish outer layer. The famous Statue of Liberty in New York is made of 300 pieces of copper, fitted together. Its green covering layer gives the metal a pleasing appearance and should make it last a long time.

# 8.

# Fuel for the Human Engine

Your body is like an engine. The food you eat is the fuel that keeps your body alive and active. It gives you energy for work and play, just as the fuel burned by an engine enables it to pull a train, hoist a load or run machinery. All we ask of a steam or gasoline engine is that it should run smoothly and efficiently. When a part wears out, we shut the engine down and repair it; but the human body must keep running for a lifetime, repairing itself as it goes along.

**Food is fuel for the human body.**

Food is burned (oxidized) in the body just as truly as coal, oil or gasoline is burned in an engine, but the chemical actions in living things are far more complicated. Certainly there is nothing more important to us than the chemistry of plants and animals. Our lives and health depend on this branch of science, which is called *biochemistry*.

Early in human history, whenever people became hungry they ate almost anything that happened to be available. In many parts of the world, even now, savages eat such things as crocodile meat, bats, caterpillars and grasshoppers. In civilized lands we often follow our natural habits and appetites in choosing food; but we know, too, that there are certain rules for choosing a wholesome, well-balanced diet. In the United States we are very lucky to have a healthful variety of appetizing foods that almost everybody can afford.

Chemists have found that certain kinds of food substances are necessary to nourish the body. One important group includes sugar and starch. These are compounds of carbon, hydrogen and oxygen, and are called *carbohydrates*.

There are many kinds of sugar. *Glucose* (GLOO-kohs) which is found in the juice of some fruits, is $C_6H_{12}O_6$; while the *sucrose* (*SOO-krohs*) in the sugar

| | | | |
|---|---|---|---|
| Starch | $C_6$ | $H_{10}$ | $O_5$ |
| Water | | $H_2$ | $O$ |
| Glucose | $C_6$ | $H_{12}$ | $O_6$ |

bowl on your breakfast table is a little more complicated chemically. Its formula is $C_{12}H_{22}O_{11}$. There are other sugars, each with its own chemical formula, in honey, vegetables and milk. Starch, which has the formula

$C_6H_{10}O_5$; is found in such foods as bread, potatoes, corn, rice and cereals.

In order to be used by the body, starch and sugar must somehow get into the blood stream. Sugars can do this easily because they dissolve in water and pass right through the side of the intestines to the blood vessels that are all around it. But starch must be changed into sugar before it can dissolve. The digestive juices do this for us just by tacking a water molecule onto each starch molecule. The glucose can then be carried into the blood stream like any sugar.

Carbohydrates give us most of our body heat and energy, and the heat comes from the oxidation, or slow burning, of food. Oxygen from the air we breathe gets into the blood stream by way of the lungs, where it combines with sugars to produce carbon dioxide and water (which are not used), and heat. Another kind of food substances, called *fats*, are furnished mainly by foods like butter and vegetable oils. They, too, can be oxidized in the body. One important thing fats do for us is to carry some of the vitamins to different parts of the body.

A pound of any certain kind of food will give off a certain amount of heat energy, whether it is burned in

1 oz. Scrambled egg = ¼ oz. Coal

1 oz. Doughnut = ½ oz. Coal

1 oz. Apple = ¹/₁₂ oz. Coal

1 oz. Butter = 1 oz. Coal

the body or outside of it. Scientists test various foods for their heat value by burning them in a special oven. They rate the foods in calories. For example, here is the amount of heat you can get from one ounce of each of these foods:

| Food | Calories |
|---|---|
| Scrambled egg | 63 |
| Doughnut | 132 |
| Apple | 19 |
| Butter | 240 |

The average person uses about 2,500 calories each day. If you eat much more than you need, the extra part is not burned up. Instead, it is stored as a layer of fat under your skin; so you see why people who are stout have to "watch their calories."

Now we come to the very important protein (*PRO-tee-in*) foods. All parts of your body are made up of tiny *cells*; and as your body grows, new cells are added. Proteins are necessary for growth and for repairing worn-out and damaged cells. We get large amounts of protein in milk, cheese, eggs, meat and fish, and smaller amounts from wheat, beans and peas. Chemically, proteins are very complicated molecules containing carbon, hydrogen, oxygen and nitrogen. Some contain sulfur and

Milk, cheese, eggs, meat and fish are high in protein.

phosphorus too. Altogether, there may be hundreds or even thousands of atoms in a single protein molecule.

In addition to the three kinds of food—carbohydrates, fats and proteins—the body needs certain *minerals* for regulating its action, helping the circulation of the blood and building strong bones and teeth. These minerals give you elements such as calcium, phosphorus and iron. Your diet must include the correct balance of mineral foods for good health.

Milk and cheese are good sources of the calcium and phosphorus needed especially by the bones and teeth. Phosphorus is also used to help build the muscles, nerves and brain. Iron is found in body cells of every kind. Liver is the richest food source of iron. Oysters, meat, peas, beans, eggs and fish are also important. The red blood cells contain a very important iron compound called *hemoglobin* (*HEE-moh-GLOW-bin*) that carries oxygen from the lungs to the various parts of the body.

Ordinary salt (sodium chloride) is always present in the blood and other liquids of the body. In the stomach, some of it is changed to hydrochloric acid (HCl), which is needed for digestion. Iodine is another element that must be taken in with food if the body is to work and grow properly. Sea foods can give us much of this element, but to get enough iodine you probably use iodized table salt at home, which is ordinary NaCl with some sodium iodide (NaI) added.

In talking about the chemistry of foods, we must not forget one of the most important substances of all—water. Although it does not give us energy or build body cells, water is absolutely necessary. It dissolves other materials so they can be sent to all parts of the body, and it helps carry away waste products.

It may surprise you to find out that many foods are made up mostly of water. More than half the weight of lean meat is water, and some vegetables and fruits are about 95 per cent water. Milk, which is called the most perfect food because it contains so many of the needed substances, is nearly nine-tenths water. About two-thirds of the weight of your body is water; so you see why it is important to drink plenty of liquids every day.

Do you know that it is possible to eat large amounts of food and still starve? You may be eating a good mixture of different kinds of foods furnishing all the *calories* you need, yet lacking certain necessary *substances*. About fifty years ago scientists began to realize that foods contain tiny amounts of other things that the body needs for good health. Later they called these substances

Lean meat / 62% Water

String beans 89% Water

Potato 78% Water

Milk 88% Water

Cucumber

96% Water

**Many foods are made up mostly of water.**

*vitamins* and named them by the letters of the alphabet.

In the early days of the clipper ships, sailors who went on long voyages would often get a dangerous disease called scurvy. Just 200 years ago, a doctor in the British navy found that eating fresh fruits and vegetables would cure this disease. It was the first time people recognized that a definite sickness could result when something was *missing* from the diet.

Nowadays this scurvy-preventing material is called *Vitamin C*, and it can be manufactured in large quantities and added to other foods because chemists have worked out its formula: $C_6H_8O_6$. Oranges, lemons, cabbage, tur-

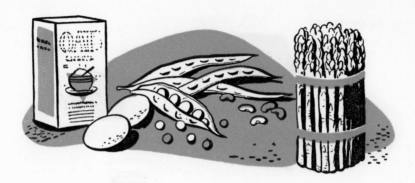

Foods such as these give us most of our Vitamin B₁.

nips and tomatoes are some natural foods containing large amounts of Vitamin C. Like all vitamins, it cannot be stored very long in the body but must be replaced all the time. Now you can see one reason why a glass of orange juice or a half grapefruit is part of a good breakfast.

Another vitamin was traced down from an exciting discovery made by a Dutch physician, Dr. Eijkman, working in far-away Java. Thousands of natives were falling ill of a dreadful, crippling disease called beriberi. Dr. Eijkman began to study the diet of these people to see if he could find some clue to the cause of their sickness. He knew that the natives lived mostly on rice which had the outer husk removed; so he tried an experiment. He fed nothing but this white rice to a flock

Foods such as these give us most of our Vitamin B₂.

of healthy chickens. Surely enough, these chickens, which were lively and active a short time before, soon became ill and weak with beriberi.

Now for the test. The doctor fed them the brown husks that had been scraped off the rice. Within a few days every chicken was well and strong again. Dr. Eijkman did not know exactly what magic substance the rice husks had in them, but he had found the secret of beriberi. He asked the Dutch government to forbid the natives to eat white rice, and soon the horrible disease was under control.

Before long, scientists in all parts of the world were tracking down other vitamins to learn about their chemistry and how to make them. Dr. Eijkman's cure for beriberi proved to be a compound now called *Vita-*

*min* $B_1$, having the formula $C_{12}H_{18}N_4Cl_2OS$. This compound is also known as *thiamin* (*THIGH-uh-min*) *hydrochloride*. It takes nearly a hundred *tons* of rice husks to give a single *ounce* of Vitamin $B_1$. Fortunately, we need only very tiny amounts of each of the vitamins daily—less than one ten-thousandth of an ounce. If you eat enough cereals, peas, beans, eggs and tomatoes, you get a good supply of Vitamin $B_1$. This keeps your nerves in good condition and helps appetite and digestion.

Another vitamin that helps you grow, keeps you strong and active and even protects you against some eye diseases, is called *Vitamin A*. It is found in foods like milk, butter, eggs, green vegetables, corn and carrots. The structural formula shows that a molecule of Vitamin A is fairly complicated.

The formula for a Vitamin A molecule is very complicated.

Foods such as these give us most of our Vitamin C.

*Vitamin D* is sometimes called the "sunshine vitamin" because it can be formed right in your skin by the action of sunlight. This compound helps build calcium and other minerals into the bones and teeth. If the bones do not take up minerals properly, they become soft; and a disease called rickets may be the result. Ordinary foods do not have much of this vitamin; so it is important for you to get as much sunshine as you can. It may be that the milk you get from the dairy is marked, "Irradiated Vitamin D." This means that before bottling, the milk was placed under powerful lamps to form Vitamin D in it.

The livers of fish such as cod and halibut are rich in Vitamins A and D. Doctors often give young children fish liver oils to supply plenty of these vitamins.

The subject of vitamins is not a simple one. Bio-chemists are finding out more about it all the time. Of the several other vitamins now known, at least one other should be mentioned, and this is *Vitamin B₂*, which is also called *riboflavin* (*ri-bo-FLA-vin*). It keeps the skin, eyes and hair healthy, and it is plentiful in meat, milk and eggs. Some of the cereals you eat may be marked, "with thiamin and riboflavin added."

While it is true that we can buy most of the important vitamins in the form of pills at the drug store, the best, safest and cheapest way to get them is by eating the proper foods. And besides, eating is much more fun than taking pills!

# 9.

# Chemicals That Cure

Because germs cause disease, it is important to keep these tiny creatures from entering the body with our food, with the air we breathe or through cuts in the skin. Most germs are really very small plants called bacteria. Unlike ordinary plants, they are not green, and some are so small they cannot be seen even with the most powerful microscopes.

Not all bacteria are harmful. In fact we could not get along without certain kinds. There are bacteria that help

1/10,000 inch

**Through a microscope you can see many kinds of bacteria.**

plants grow, others that get rid of dead animals and plants by making them decay, and some that live in soil and make it better for growing crops. Bacteria in the intestines of a cow make it possible for the animal to digest the grass it eats. Still other kinds of bacteria are useful in making cheese. Yeast is made up of slightly larger plants, something like bacteria, that produce a chemical which can change sugar to alcohol. In fact, all bacteria do their work by causing chemical changes, and that is why the biochemist is interested in them.

It is hard to believe that until less than a hundred years ago people did not know that diseases were caused by germs. Then Louis Pasteur, a French chemist, found that bacteria were everywhere, and that when certain kinds entered a plant or animal they were able to grow and cause disease there.

In England, a surgeon named Joseph Lister thought that such bacteria might be the reason for so many infections and deaths after surgical operations. In those days, anyone who went to a hospital for even a minor operation was in great danger of getting "blood poisoning." Doctors wore their ordinary dusty street clothes when they operated, and simply rinsed off their instruments with water afterwards. Lister sprayed the air of the operating rooms with carbolic acid and made sure that the surgeon washed his hands, instruments and bandages

Pasteur found that bacteria were everywhere.

with carbolic acid solution, too. The number of cases of blood poisoning dropped off at once. Lister had discovered the use of *antiseptics* and also proved that Pasteur was right about germs being the cause of disease.

Since that time, chemists have given us better antiseptics such as iodine, alcohol, formalin, mercurochrome and many others. Wound infections hardly ever happen in our hospitals now. And if one should get started, there are new and powerful drugs to stop it quickly.

Lister and other scientists began to wonder if chemicals might be used to destroy germs inside the human body as well as outside. Most doctors thought this would be impossible, but a clever German chemist, Paul Ehrlich, refused to be discouraged by the failures of others. He started with an antiseptic containing the

This is a molecule of carbolic acid.

element arsenic, and changed the molecule of this compound again and again. Strangely enough, these compounds are also dyes. They are made from coal tar, a sticky substance produced when soft coal is heated to make coke.

After more than six hundred failures, Dr. Ehrlich finally made a drug that could kill certain bacteria without harming the patient. He not only made one of the greatest discoveries in the history of medicine, but also invented a new word to describe this kind of treatment. The word is *chemotherapy* (*kem-oh-THER-uh-pe*), meaning "curing by means of chemicals."

Before the time of Dr. Ehrlich's discovery, doctors believed that helpful drugs could be obtained only from plants, but now they began to search for other mineral drugs, especially among the many coal-tar dyes. They found remedies for many diseases that were considered incurable up to that time. About twenty years ago, the chemicals belonging to the *sulfa* family were found to be very powerful, even against such "tough" bacteria as the ones causing pneumonia, blood poisoning and some ear and throat infections. *Sulfanilamide* (*sul-fah-NIL-uh-mide*) and *sulfathiazole* (*sul-fah-THI-uh-zol*) are two that you may have heard of. Some of the sulfa

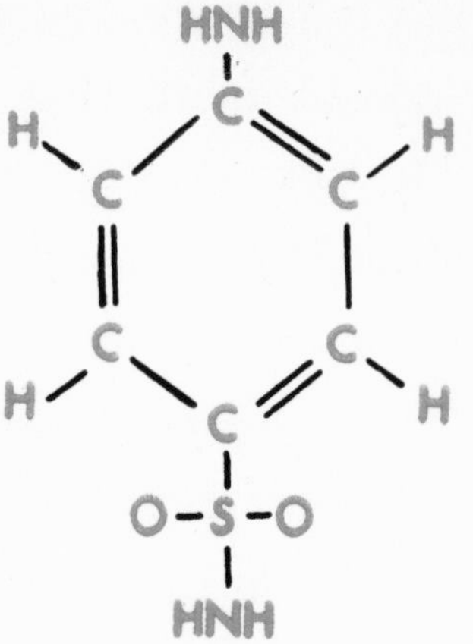

HNH
|
C

H   C       C   H

C           C

H   C       C   H

C
|
O–S–O
|
HNH

**This is a molecule of sulfanilamide.**

drugs can be taken as pills, while others can be smeared directly on cuts and burns.

The interesting thing about the sulfa chemicals is that they are not able to kill bacteria on a dish in the laboratory but can stop germs from growing only in or on the body itself. Scientists think that this is because sulfa drugs have the power to soften the outer parts of bacteria, giving the cells and chemicals in our blood a chance to attack the germs and finish them off.

One of the most curious facts about some important medicines is that they come from very strange materials. You learned that sticky, disagreeable coal tar gives lifesaving sulfa drugs, and that important vitamins come from rice husks and fish livers. And now we find that some of the most valuable of all germ killers come from mold, something like the yellow or greenish fuzz that forms on a piece of stale bread or cheese.

It all came about as a result of an accidental discovery by an English scientist, Dr. Alexander Fleming. By this time you realize that such "accidents" happen only to people who are prepared to recognize their importance, and who know how to follow up a lucky "break."

One day Dr. Fleming's assistant brought him a plate on which a colony of dangerous bacteria were being grown. (In the laboratory, a crop of germs is raised by putting a few bacteria on a plate of gelatin and letting them grow.) "This plate is spoiled," said the assistant. "Some mold accidentally formed on it and I'll have to throw it away."

Penicillin mold in a dish of gelatin destroyed the bacteria.

Dr. Fleming was ready to agree. Then he looked at the dish again. "Hold on!" he said excitedly. "The germs all *around* the mold are gone! Whatever destroyed them must have come from that fluffy blue-green mold."

There was much work still to be done. Other molds, relatives of the one on the dish, were tried on many kinds of bacteria. More scientists joined in the work. Finally they found that the mold got its germ-fighting power from a chemical that it produced in very small amounts. It was decided to call the new drug *penicillin* (*pen-uh-SILL-in*), after the name of the blue-green mold.

By this time World War II was on, and the armed forces were in great need of this new germ killer. But it could not be produced fast enough in England. So some of the mold was brought to the United States where a way was found to make penicillin in large quantities. Today it is made in huge 15,000-gallon steel tanks, and supplies are on hand in every drug store and hospital. Penicillin has become one of our best weapons against bacteria. It really deserves the popular name of "wonder drug."

The amazing results that doctors got with sulfa drugs and penicillin encouraged them to search for other drugs that might help fight some of the diseases still giving them great trouble. One of the worst of these is tuberculosis. Only a short time ago, over 50,000 people were dying of it every year in the United States. In the last ten years, this number has been cut down by one-third, mostly as a result of discovering some new germ killers in the soil.

The first one of these that worked properly was named *streptomycin* (*strep-toe-MY-sin*). It was discovered by the American scientist Dr. Selman Waksman in 1944, after he had patiently made more than 10,000 tests. He found that this compound could kill many kinds of germs that penicillin did not affect. Most important of all, it has been used with some success in treating tuberculosis.

Our smallest and most dangerous germ enemies are the queer ones of the *virus* (*VI-russ*) family. They are

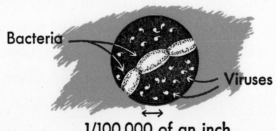

Bacteria

Viruses

←→ 1/100,000 of an inch

With an electron microscope you can see bacteria and viruses.

only a few millionths of an inch across and cannot be seen except with an *electron microscope*. Scientists know that a virus can grow only when it is inside the body, but they are not even sure whether it is a plant or a tiny animal.

Many diseases, including measles, influenza, polio and the common cold, are caused by viruses. Just a few years ago, another virus killer called *chloromycetin* (*klo-row-MY-set-in*) was discovered in some soil from South America. Chloromycetin can destroy the virus of a dreadful sickness called typhus, and now it can be made directly in a chemical laboratory in large amounts. An even newer virus fighter, *aureomycin* (*oh-ree-oh-MY-sin*), is used to treat undulant fever and amebic dysentery.

Almost every day we hear of the discovery of still other wonder drugs. There is great hope that one may soon be found that cures or prevents polio, and it may even turn out that cancer will some day be beaten by a chemical. Thanks largely to penicillin, sulfa and the other wonder drugs, the number of deaths from pneumonia, blood poisoning, appendicitis and other serious illnesses has been cut down to a fraction of what it was only ten years ago.

Aureomycin is prepared in great sheets.

Today we are not only healthier but live longer than people did in the past. A person born at the time of your grandparents could expect to live on the average about forty-nine years. This figure is now up to sixty-seven years, and most of the gain has come since the time you yourself were born. Doctors say that chemotherapy has done more for our health in the past twenty years than all the improvements in the last four thousand years.

# 10.

# Chemistry on the Farm

Although you may not have thought of it in that way,
a farm is really a kind of chemical factory, and the farmer
something of a chemist. People who study scientific farming at an agricultural college must study a great deal about
chemistry. But even without such training, farmers have
learned many chemical facts through experience handed
down from one generation to the next for thousands of
years.

Everything we eat depends on plants, for they alone

have the secret of manufacturing certain necessary chemicals such as sugars and proteins (see Chapter 8). Every animal must rely on plant life for its existence, either by feeding on plants themselves or on plant-eating animals.

The farmer must battle constantly against the forces of nature in order to feed the people of the world. In spite of frost, windstorms, drought, harmful insects and other enemies that threaten to destroy his crops, he must continue to provide nourishment for people and animals. But the farmer is not alone in the fight against starvation. The countless trillions of bacteria in the soil are his allies. Without their help, his job would be impossible, as you will see.

When food crops or other plants are taken from the ground, the chemicals of which they are made must be put back into the soil in order to keep it fertile. The farmer can do this by adding a *fertilizer* such as manure, dried fish, bone, garbage, or some prepared chemical mixture. The most important elements in a complete fertilizer are nitrogen, phosphorus and potassium, all needed by growing plants. However, before the plants can use these elements they must be worked on by bacteria. And these bacteria themselves need still other elements such as iron, copper, magnesium and sulfur in order to live. So when the farmer spreads fertilizer, he is not only providing for his crops but is feeding his bacteria helpers at the same time.

Bacteria, like other workers, specialize in certain jobs. Some are able to break down proteins, sugars and starches. Others can attack cellulose and fats. When soil bacteria digest these materials, they produce such things as hydrogen, methane, carbon dioxide and ammonia. In the huge, well-organized chemical factory that we have in the soil, some bacteria have the task of partly oxidizing certain chemicals. After this others take over and change these materials further.

In Chapter 8 it was explained that proteins are needed in our food because all the cells of the body are made from such compounds. One of the necessary elements that go to make up proteins is nitrogen. But plants and animals cannot take nitrogen right out of the air for this purpose. They can build their needed proteins only by starting with nitrogen compounds.

There is a special kind of bacteria in the soil that *is* able to take nitrogen out of the air and *fix* it, which means making it combine with other elements. Some varieties of nitrogen-fixing bacteria team up with green plants such as peas, beans, clover and alfalfa by settling down in the roots of these plants. The plant then builds little grape-like clusters of root material around the bacteria and furnishes the sugars which they need in order to live. In return, the bacteria form proteins out of nitrogen gas from the air or

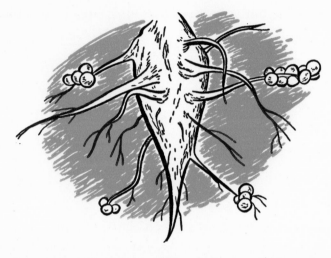

Some plants build grape-like clusters on their roots.

the soil, and the plant builds some of these proteins into its own cells. Altogether, this wonderful partnership is what makes life possible for plants, and in turn for animals too.

Clover and alfalfa produce crop after crop without replanting. If these crops are plowed under, the fixed nitrogen in the plants is returned to the soil. This makes the soil rich enough to grow other kinds of crops without the addition of any other nitrogen fertilizer. Because of this the farmer usually *rotates* his crops. One year he plants clover in a field, then plows it into the soil. The following years he may plant corn, oats, barley and peas. Then he starts once more with clover and goes through the list again.

Chemists have found ways of fixing nitrogen without the help of bacteria. Almost all artificial fertilizers are made by forcing nitrogen and hydrogen gases to combine directly to form ammonia, $NH_3$. This was done for the first time by German chemists just before World War I. Unfortunately, the discovery made it possible not only to produce plant foods but also to manufacture explosives for war.

The complicated chemical actions that take place among plants, animals and bacteria are all part of a great round of happenings called the *nitrogen cycle*. You will be able to follow this cycle with the help of the picture.

First of all, the leaves of plants contain a very complex green substance called *chlorophyll*. Somehow, using the energy of sunlight, chlorophyll enables the plant to combine water from the soil with carbon dioxide from the air to form starches, sugars and other important plant food. This food making is called *photosynthesis* (FO-tuh-SIN-thuh-siss). With these products, plants are then able to

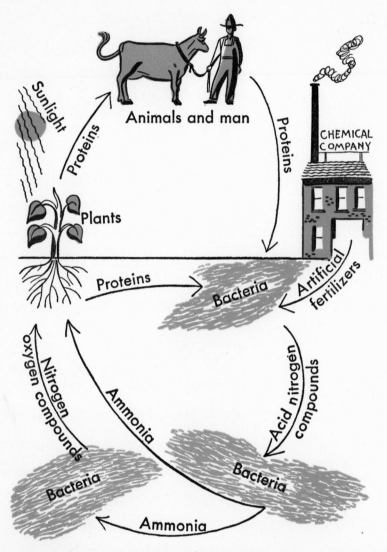

Sunlight

Proteins

Animals and man

Proteins

CHEMICAL COMPANY

Plants

Proteins

Bacteria

Artificial fertilizers

Nitrogen oxygen compounds

Ammonia

Acid nitrogen compounds

Bacteria

Bacteria

Ammonia

The complicated chemical actions that take place among plants, animals and bacteria are all part of the "nitrogen cycle."

build up proteins and fats. After animals eat and digest their food, protein waste matter is left, to be returned to the soil. Also, plant material that is not used for food can be returned to the soil direct. Artificial fertilizers may be added too, as the drawing shows.

Once back in the soil, the proteins are attacked by bacteria that change them to acid nitrogen compounds. Other bacteria then take over and form ammonia. Some of the ammonia is used directly by plants, but the rest is changed by still another kind of bacteria into compounds of nitrogen and oxygen before being taken up by the plant roots. Then comes photosynthesis, and the cycle starts all over again. So it turns out that the unpleasant processes in which organic materials rot and decay are really the ones that make life on earth possible.

Although agriculture is the oldest industry in the world, new methods are being discovered all the time. From long experience farmers have known that no artificial fertilizer is quite so good as the natural ones such as vegetable mulch and manure, but it took the chemists to discover the reason. In natural fertilizers there are tiny amounts of organic compounds called plant *hormones*. They do for plants what vitamins do for animals. Chemists are now finding out more about these substances and making them available for practical use in the soil.

During the last few years, such discoveries have led to an interesting new way of raising plants without the use of soil at all! This method is called *hydroponics* (HI-druh-PON-iks). In one way of doing it, the plants are held with their roots dipped into a tank containing the chemicals they need, and air is bubbled through the solution to furnish oxygen to the roots. Such careful control is needed that this method will probably never take the place of ordinary farming for the staple crops such as grain. But it works out well for raising certain vegetables and flowers.

Another development of the last few years is the dis-

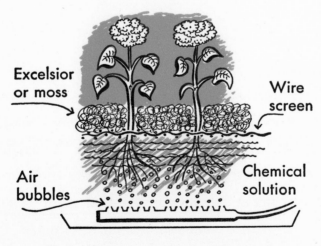

These plants are growing without soil.

covery of *soil conditioners*, such as Krilium. These are not fertilizers—their job is only to make the soil porous. If soil becomes water-soaked, it mats down into a solid mass, and no air can reach the nitrogen-fixing soil bacteria. The conditioners make the soil particles form crumbs or granules so that air can get into the spaces between them. Breaking up the soil in this way also makes it easier for roots to push outward and for sprouts to force their way upward. As a result plants grow faster and reach a larger size when the soil is treated with conditioners. Thus these compounds are beginning to be widely used by vegetable growers.

Although we think of the farm mainly in connection with food, some farm products never come to our table at all but go direct to factories where a great many other things are made from them. There is an important branch of practical chemistry, called *chemurgy* (KEM-ur-jee), that deals with the use of organic farm products in industry. Each year through this science, millions of tons of farm wastes are changed into valuable materials.

Chemurgy supplies us with an amazing variety of things. Cornstalks are used to make sound-deadening wallboard. Potatoes and grains can be worked on by bacteria and yeasts to produce alcohol, which has important commercial chemical uses. Milk, soybeans, wood pulp and animal wastes can be turned into attractive plastics with hundreds of forms and uses, as you will find in the next chapter. From peanut oil, chemists make vegetable shortening, oleomargarine, soap and explosives. Even the peanut hulls are valuable for making such things as linoleum and fiber board. Other peanut products are ink, rubber substitutes, face powder and dyes.

The great agricultural chemist George Washington Carver was able to find over three hundred uses for peanuts and sweet potatoes. Although he was born the son of a Negro slave in the South, he taught himself science and finally became one of the country's most brilliant research chemists. He showed farmers how to raise a greater variety of crops in order to improve their soil and provide them with better food.

Chemistry has brought about enormous improvements in farm methods and farm products. In return, agriculture has furnished many of the most valuable raw materials for chemical industry. The partnership between the chemist and the farmer has always been of benefit to both, and is sure to bring even more benefits in the future.

# 11.

# Fibers and Plastics

No matter where we live, we need clothing to keep us warm or to protect our bodies from sun and wind. Ages ago, people learned to make rough garments from animal skins. Later they found how to twist hairs or fibers together to make threads that could be woven into cloth.

Wool and silk have been used in this way for thousands of years, and cloth has been woven from plant fibers such as cotton and flax for almost as long a time.

Wool is the soft hair of sheep and some other animals, while silk is obtained from the cocoons of a caterpillar.

Woven cloths are known as textiles, and we use them not only for making clothing but for rugs, drapes, curtains, blankets, flags, mats and many other things. The modern textile industry relies very much on chemistry. Chemists now know about the nature of textile fibers and how to dye them thousands of beautiful colors.

In the last few years, textile chemists have accomplished something even more important. They have found how to make artificial, or synthetic, fibers that are in some ways much better than any natural ones. Synthetic means "built up" or "put together" from other materials. Today it is quite true to say that we dress in garments made of such unlikely materials as sour milk, wood, air, natural gas and coal. But before finding out

Flax

Wool

Cotton

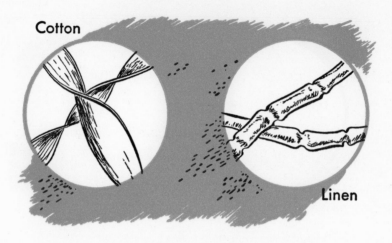

Cotton

Linen

Cotton and linen look like this in a microscope.

about the newer fibers, you should have a closer look at the older and more familiar ones.

Cotton comes first because it is used more than any other textile fiber. Thirty million bales of cotton are grown each year, and almost half of it comes from the southern part of the United States. Cotton is mostly cellulose, the material that forms the main part of wood and other plant cells. Cellulose is a carbohydrate, but chemists cannot tell the exact size of its molecules. Each one is probably made up of more than a hundred starch molecules hooked together in a long chain. Using the energy of sunshine, plants are able to make carbon dioxide combine with water to form a compound called *form-*

Wool and silk look like this in a microscope.

*aldehyde*, $CH_2O$. Then the plants go on to make larger and larger polymers out of the formaldehyde molecules —first alcohols, then sugars, starches and finally cellulose.

Linen comes from the flax plant. Like cotton, it is almost pure cellulose; but the fibers are stronger than those of cotton and have a shiny surface. Under a microscope, linen and cotton fibers are quite different in appearance, as the picture shows. A cotton fiber looks like a twisted ribbon, while linen is made of jointed tubes, like bamboo.

Wool, our most important animal fiber, is a protein compound having sulfur in it. Chemically it is very much like hair, fingernails and feathers. Under a microscope, wool fibers look like tubes covered with scales, as in the picture. If you want to tell whether a suit or a scarf contains wool, pull off a few fibers and burn them. If they burn slowly, leaving much ash, and have an odor like burned chicken feathers, the fibers are probably wool. On the other hand, cotton and linen burn easily, giving an odor like burned paper, and leave very little ash.

Silk is the strongest of all textile fibers. Like wool, it is a protein compound, but does not have sulfur in it. The silkworm, which is really the caterpillar of a certain kind of moth, produces a sticky liquid in its mouth. When this liquid comes out into the air, it hardens into a fine fiber which the silkworm spins into a cocoon.

The silkworm feeds on mulberry leaves.

The fibers can later be unwound from the cocoons and spun into threads to be woven into beautiful, soft silk cloth.

When chemists started out to make synthetic fibers, they imitated the silkworm by making a thick liquid that could be stretched out into fine threads and then made to harden. The best known artificial fiber is *rayon*, and while there are several ways of making it, the *viscose* method is used more than any other.

The starting point is cellulose obtained from wood pulp or cotton. Two chemicals, sodium hydroxide (NaOH) and carbon disulfide ($CS_2$), are used to change the fibers into a golden, syrupy liquid. The liquid is then forced through tiny holes in a metal disk. For making the thinnest rayon threads, these holes are only about 1/5,000 of an inch across. The fibers coming from the holes are not hardened in air but in a special chemical solution. They are then brought together and twisted into yarn, ready for use in weaving cloth.

Many different kinds of textiles can be made from rayon—fine, silky ones, smooth velvets or heavy cloth for making suits. It all depends on the size of the fiber and how it is prepared chemically. Rayon is also used for making cords that give strength to automobile tires,

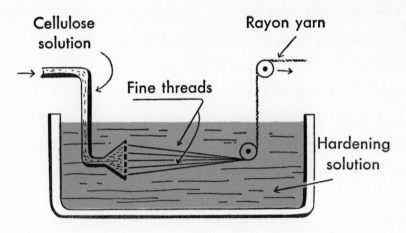

Cellulose solution

Rayon yarn

Fine threads

Hardening solution

This shows how rayon is made by the viscose process.

rubber hose, and belts that drive machinery. Chemists can now make rayon so strong that a single thread about as big across as the lead in a pencil could hold up your whole weight.

Cellophane is probably the form of rayon you know best. It is made by the viscose method, the cellulose syrup being forced through a long, narrow slit instead of through small holes. After it has been cleaned and dried, the thin sheet is wound on rolls. Cellophane is strong, flexible and transparent. It acts as a protection against moisture. This makes it useful for wrapping such things as food, candy and cigarettes.

Another kind of rayon is made by the *acetate* (*AS-*

*uh-tate*) method. Cellulose in the form of cotton fibers is again changed into a thick liquid, but this time by acetic (*uh-SEE-tik*) acid, the sour-tasting chemical in vinegar. The finished fibers are made into an artificial silk cloth called celanese.

In making rayon it is necessary to start with natural cellulose from wood or cotton, but another useful fiber called *nylon* is a completely synthetic compound made from coal, air and water. Its molecules are long, chain-like polymers containing carbon, hydrogen, oxygen and nitrogen atoms—really a protein very much like silk. Nylon can be spun into very fine, strong threads simply by melting it, forcing it through small holes and letting it harden in the air. It is easily dyed and dries quickly after washing, so it is very popular for making stockings, shirts, underwear and other articles of clothing.

During World War II nylon proved valuable in making tents, hammocks, rope and parachutes for the armed forces because, unlike most natural fibers, it does not rot and fall apart in the hot, moist air of the jungle. At home, we find such things as brush bristles, fishing lines and strings for tennis racquets made of nylon. There are several other polymer fibers that are like nylon, and each has its own uses. You may see the names *velon, orlon, saran*, or *dacron* in advertisements for window screens, curtains, shirts, suits, furniture coverings or luggage.

A third kind of artificial fiber is made of cottage cheese! This is mostly *casein* (*KAY-see-in*), the protein part of milk. Many million gallons of skim milk, with the casein in it, used to be thrown away each year. Now, much of it is changed into casein wool by making the protein molecules polymerize to form much bigger molecules. This product looks and feels very much like real wool, and is even better in some ways.

In general, anything that can be molded into various shapes is called a plastic, and so the rayon, nylon and casein wool that we have been talking about are really plastics. Common materials such as cement, glass, clay, plaster and wax are plastics. Chemists now know how to make many artificial plastics that can be shaped by heat and pressure to form an enormous variety of things —toys, phonograph records, film for your camera, dishes, buttons, and thousands of other products.

The first modern plastic was invented as a result of a shortage of big elephants in Africa and a cut finger. Here is how it happened: The hard, white ivory of elephant tusks had been used to make piano keys, ornaments and billiard balls. At about the time of our Civil

Parachutes and rope are often made from nylon.

War, hunters in Africa were not finding many of the large elephants whose tusks were big enough for making billiard balls. As a result, an American company offered a prize of $10,000 to anyone who could make a substitute for ivory billiard balls.

A printer named John Hyatt happened to cut his finger one day, and he went to get some collodion to put on the wound. Collodion is a cellulose solution, not very different from the ones you have just been reading about. When he opened the medicine cabinet, Hyatt found that the collodion had spilled onto the shelf and hardened. Out of curiosity, he pulled away some of the rubbery mass and rolled it between his fingers to form a smooth ball. Then he remembered reading about the prize for an ivory substitute, and he and his brother went to work in their home chemical laboratory.

Finally they were able to produce a new material, called *celluloid*. It failed to win the prize because it did not prove suitable for making billiard balls, but it could be used for many other things. In this way, the first synthetic plastic material was invented.

Celluloid has one great disadvantage—it burns very easily—and so it is no longer used very much. But its place is being taken by many other wonderful materials.

Different types of plastics are used for different purposes. One kind, made from phenol ($C_6H_6O$) and formaldehyde ($CH_2O$), was invented more than fifty years ago. The commonest form, called bakelite, can be

given a smooth, hard finish that makes it useful for many purposes. The telephone instrument in your home is pressed from this material. Bakelite is also made into pot handles, bottle caps, electric switch handles, and so on.

There are also the *vinyl* (*VI-nil*) plastics, which are polymers of molecules such as vinyl acetate, $C_4H_6O_2$; and this in turn is made from the simpler molecule of acetylene, $C_2H_2$. Vinyl plastics are tough, strong and transparent. One material of this group, called *vinylite*, is used to stick together two layers of glass to make safety glass for automobile windshields. If this glass should happen to shatter, the fragments will stick to the sheet of plastic instead of scattering dangerously. Other vinyl plastics serve as coatings for food containers, electric wire, and cloth; and one kind makes a very strong glue.

Your dentist may use a clever lamp fitted with a plastic rod in order to get light into your mouth without putting the hot lamp itself too close to you. Light travels along the crystal-clear *lucite* (*LOO-site*) rod like water along a pipe. Lucite belongs to the *acrylic* (*uh-KRIL-ik*) plastics, which are clear and glasslike. The starting point for making them is again acetylene. The transparent nose

Light can be "piped" along a rod of lucite.

of a fighter plane is made of another acrylic plastic, called *plexiglas*. The manufacturers turn out beautifully colored acrylic plastics in sheets, tubes and rods from which many useful and ornamental articles are made.

Are you finding it hard to keep in mind all the plastics that have been described so far? If so, do not worry. Chemists themselves have a hard time keeping track of them all. There are more than 5,000 kinds, and new ones are being invented all the time.

One final group will be mentioned—the *nitrogen plastics*. You already met one of them in the form of casein plastic, but there are others that are good for making buckles, ornaments and buttons. Nitrogen plastics can also be made from such unusual materials as soybeans, animal wastes, egg white and coffee beans.

In less than a hundred years, plastics have become one of the biggest products of the chemical industry. Nearly a million tons of these materials are manufactured each year. They have taken the place of other materials for many purposes, for we now have plastics that look like wood or metal, and others that look like marble, glass or leather.

In most cases where plastics have replaced another material, the result has been an improved product. When metal is used to make a toy, a camera body or a radio cabinet, it is necessary to cut, shape or stamp the material. In addition, it may have to be welded, soldered or riveted. However, when plastic is used, the article often can be formed simply by a single pressing or molding operation.

Things made of plastic are usually lighter in weight than when made of metal and have the additional advantage that they can be colored all the way through instead of having only a surface coat of paint. Another point in favor of plastics is that they can be made from farm products, while metals come from ores that must first be located and then removed from the ground, usually with great trouble and expense.

Wherever you happen to be, indoors or out, look around and see for yourself how these bright, gleaming materials make so many ordinary things more beautiful and colorful, as well as more useful and efficient.

# 12.

# Rubber

Many centuries ago, Indians in Central and South America found a strange jungle tree. When they cut into its bark, big drops of a milky liquid came out. Because these drops looked like tears, the tree was named "weeping wood." The Indians found that the liquid would harden into a queer, gummy substance that bounced when it hit the ground.

Not long after the discovery of America, Spanish explorers in Mexico found the Aztec Indians using a bouncing ball to play a game somewhat like basketball. When they returned to Europe, travelers brought pieces of the strange gum with them. Some of it was seen by Joseph Priestly. He remarked, "I have seen a substance excellently adapted to the purpose of wiping from paper the marks of a black lead pencil." From its use in rubbing out pencil marks, the gum received its name, *rubber*.

In Europe and in this country, people were beginning to wonder if rubber could be put to work in other ways. Cloth coated with the gum was found to be waterproof, but it became sticky in hot weather, and hard and stiff when cold. Even so, factories started to make rubber shoes, hose, wagon covers and other articles.

The problem of making rubber firm and pliable was solved by an American inventor, Charles Goodyear, through one of those "lucky accidents" that occasionally happen. One day, while working with a mixture of sulfur and rubber, Goodyear spilled some of it on a hot stove. The rubber became firm and yet stayed elastic, and Goodyear knew he was on the right track. After more experiments, he patented *vulcanized rubber*, named after Vulcan, the Roman god of fire. This invention created a great demand for rubber; and huge planta-

Liquid rubber is collected in a cup, drop by drop.

tions of rubber trees were started in the hot, moist countries of the Far East and South America.

Liquid rubber, which is called *latex* (*LAY-tex*), comes mostly from the Para rubber tree which grows to a height of more than fifty feet. Only about one-third of the liquid is rubber and the rest is water.

A tree is "tapped" by cutting into the bark, and the liquid is collected in a cup, drop by drop. Workers go from one tree to the next, making new cuts and emptying the cups of latex. They bring the gathered latex to a

Crepe rubber comes through in crinkled sheets.

central place where it is strained to remove dirt. Then acid is added to make the small rubber particles clump together in a soft mass like dough. Next it is put through rollers that squeeze the water out. The rubber comes through in crinkled sheets that look something like crepe paper; so it is called crepe rubber. This can be used directly for making crepe-soled sport shoes. On some plantations, the rolled sheets are hung in a smokehouse to dry before they are shipped to the rubber goods factories.

Some of the latex is kept liquid and shipped in tanks. It is then molded to make rubber goods like gloves, bathing caps and sheets. However, most rubber articles are made from vulcanized rubber. The raw rubber is kneaded like dough, and sulfur and certain fillers are added. These fillers not only make the final product better but also give it color. For instance, the pale yellow crude rubber is changed to the shiny black kind used for making rubber hose and tires by putting in some carbon black, which is very fine carbon powder. Then the mixture is molded or pressed into the shape wanted and vulcanized with heat and strong pressure.

Three-quarters of the world's rubber is used for making automobile tires and tubes. The casing, or main part of the tire, is built up from flat rubber strips into

A rubber tire is put into a mold and vulcanized.

which cotton, rayon or nylon cords have been pressed to give the rubber strength. The tire is put into a mold and vulcanized, after which it is trimmed and cleaned.

During World War II the Japanese invaded the rubber-producing countries of the Far East, and our supply of natural rubber was cut off. This was just at the time we needed so much of it for tires for trucks, jeeps and planes, as well as for making balloons, life rafts and storage batteries.

But our chemists were not caught unprepared. For many years they had been studying the chemistry of natural rubber and experimenting with ways of making substitutes for it. They knew that rubber is a hydrocarbon containing eight hydrogen atoms to every five carbon atoms. In fact, when the hydrocarbon $C_5H_8$,

This is a small part of a molecule of natural rubber.

which is called *isoprene* (*I-suh-preen*), is allowed to stand, it changes to a rubbery substance by forming a polymer.

Chemists believe that each molecule of natural rubber is a tremendously long chain of as many as 10,000 of these isoprene groups hooked together. Here you see a flat diagram of part of such a chain. Actually it twists every which way in space, like a kinky piece of wire, and this is probably what gives rubber its springiness.

These long molecules are all tangled together, forming a sort of network. When rubber is vulcanized, the sulfur atoms hook the rubber molecules together at many places, making the mass of rubber strong and firm. If

Vulcanizing makes the long rubber molecules hook together.

there are only a few of these "knots" the rubber is soft and elastic, while if there are a great many, it becomes dense and stiff like the hard rubber used in making combs.

Knowing this much, chemists realized that if they were to discover how to make synthetic rubber they would have to find a way to build long, chainlike polymers. The first good rubber substitute they succeeded in making was called *neoprene* (*NEE-o-preen*). It is made from acetylene ($C_2H_2$) and hydrochloric acid (HCl). Although it costs more than natural rubber, neoprene does not break down as easily when exposed to gasoline, oil, sunlight or air.

Even before the war, the United States government had been helping some of the rubber companies to experiment with an artificial rubber called *Buna S* (*BUE-nah-ESS*), made from two chemicals called *butadiene* (*bue-tuh-DIE-een*), and *styrene* (*STY-reen*), so that by the time the Japanese cut off our main supply of natural rubber, dozens of new factories were making enough Buna S for our war needs.

Buna S proved so useful that after the war most companies kept on making it, especially for heavy-duty automobile and truck tires. Of all the rubber substitutes we

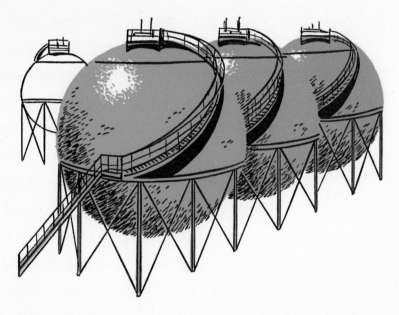

**Butadiene is stored under pressure in huge round tanks.**

have, Buna S is the most widely used and is most like natural rubber. Now more than four-fifths of all the synthetic rubber made in this country is Buna S.

Chemists can make more than sixty kinds of rubber substitutes, but the manufacturers do not like to call them "substitutes" because the new materials have some uses that natural rubber never had. Instead, they prefer to speak of all rubber-like substances as *elastomers*.

*Butyl* (*BUE-til*) is a very good elastomer that can hold air ten times as long as natural rubber. This makes it the ideal material for inner tubes of tires. *Koroseal* is a rubbery polymer of vinyl chloride. It is not so stretchable as most elastomers, but it does not burn easily and can be readily dyed in many colors. Shower curtains, belts, raincoats and umbrellas are some of the things now made of koroseal.

In the spring every year we pack our woolen clothes and blankets away in mothballs. In the same way, at the end of a war, some of our tanks, guns and even whole battleships are—as we say—"put away in mothballs." Of course, the purpose is not to protect them against moths, but against rust and tarnish. This is often done by spraying the metal parts with an elastomer called *thiokol* (*THIGH-oh-coal*). This material is not so strong as

Machinery can be protected by spraying on synthetic rubber.

natural rubber, but is not so easily attacked by gasoline, grease or other chemicals. It is sprayed on in the form of a gummy liquid and dries to form a tough coating that protects machinery while it is in storage or being shipped. Thiokol is also put to work in the form of rollers for spreading ink over the type in a printing press.

None of the dozens of elastomers that chemists have been able to make is exactly like natural rubber, but that does not worry them. They are too busy making special elastomers for new jobs. Some of these materials are good for putting under heavy machinery to cushion the vibration. Others can be used to make protective clothing for people who work with strong chemicals. "Foam rubber" is made by whipping air into the latex with an electric beater very much like the one used to whip cream in the kitchen. Mattresses, pillows and chair cushions are some of the things made from foam rubber.

Certain airplane parts are made of special elastomers which stay strong and flexible even when the temperature drops to nearly a hundred degrees below zero high over the North Pole.

The scientists and engineers who work with elastomers say that many new uses for these valuable materials are sure to be found. They even believe that before long we will travel over rubber roads in cars that not only use rubber tires but have rubber springs and even rubber bodies.

# 13.

# More Good Things From Chemistry

From what you have read so far, perhaps you now have a better understanding of the fact that chemistry is all around us and that it affects our lives in many ways. Of course we have hardly begun to tell all that is known about chemistry and its uses. Far from it! No single book, nor even a collection of books, could do that. And besides, chemistry is growing at such a fast rate that every day brings important new discoveries.

Just to round out our story of how chemistry works

for humanity, we will tell a little about some important branches of this science that have not yet been mentioned.

Chemists have helped develop new kinds of paint.

PAINTS: Spread a brushful of water on a wall and it will dry by evaporating away. However, if you spread a brushful of paint on the wall, it dries by a chemical action in which the oil in the paint oxidizes to form a tough skin. Mixed in with the oil is a *paint base*, such as white lead or zinc oxide, which prevents the covered surface from showing through. If the paint is to be any shade but white, coloring compounds are added.

Chemists working in this industry have found ways of making many new products in the last few years. We now have plastic paints and rubber-base paints which are weatherproof, casein paints that dissolve in water, and even fireproof paints.

DYES: Up to about a hundred years ago, all our dyes came from plants, animals or the soil. They were very expensive and generally of poor quality. Now nearly all of them are made from coal tar by complicated chemical methods. There are about 5,000 different dyes now in use for coloring cloth. To be acceptable, a dye must be harmless to cloth, and must not wash out or fade.

**Vessels of dye are tested on a steam table.**

Other kinds of dyes are used for coloring shoe polish, candles, soap, candy and countless other things.

LEATHER: This product has been made for thousands of years, ever since it was discovered that smoke would preserve animal skins so they could be used for clothing and other purposes. Later, it was found that a chemical in the bark of certain trees not only did the job better than smoke, but also removed the hairs from the skin.

Leather is made just about the same way today. The skins are soaked in acid, which makes them swell up, after which they go into tanks containing bark from trees. A chemical in the bark, called tannin, slowly changes the hides into leather. A newer and quicker method, using chromium compounds instead of tannin, is also widely used.

Marshmallow is mixed in this stainless steel beater.

There are now many leather substitutes made by coating cloth with plastics, but natural leather is still used for making most of our luggage, shoes, belts, gloves and furniture coverings.

CANDY: This is certainly the tastiest branch of the

chemical industry! Chemists are constantly watching over the blending of sugars with other carbohydrate foods such as syrups, honey and molasses, or with milk products and flavorings, to make up the delicious candies that we all enjoy. More than two and a half billion pounds of candy are eaten in the United States every year.

**Glass is melted in great pots.**

GLASS: This is our oldest plastic, and it has more uses today than ever before. It is made by melting silica sand (silicon dioxide, $SiO_2$), usually with soda or lime added. Many kinds of glass are made for different purposes such as windowpanes, lenses and tableware. *Spun glass* is made by pulling melted glass into very fine threads. Cloth woven from these threads is strong and flexible

133

**Soap is churned into a smooth mass.**

and is not affected by air, water or chemicals. It is also fireproof and so is often used for curtains and draperies.

SOAP: The average American family uses over a hundred pounds of soap each year. Soap is an organic compound made by boiling fat and lye (NaOH) together in huge kettles that hold as much as 175 tons. Next, salt is added to remove impurities, after which the soap is churned into a smooth mass. At the same time, coloring and perfumes are added. After the mixture has been rolled into sheets, it is stamped into separate cakes.

Soap cleans things by breaking up the film of grease

that holds dirt in place, so that the dirt can be rinsed away. Anything that cleanses is called a *detergent*, but in the last few years this name has been used mainly for the new chemical cleaners that are made from petroleum oils instead of animal or vegetable fats. These synthetic detergents seem to be better than ordinary soap because they work more easily and form less scum.

COSMETICS: These chemical products are of great interest to girls and women because they include face powder, rouge, skin creams and hair preparations. Face powder may contain chalk, talc, zinc oxide, powdered clay, starch, coloring matter and perfume. Lipstick is made of beeswax mixed with red coal-tar dyes. An oil is added to soften the wax. Cold cream is a frothy mixture of water with oil—sometimes lanolin, a grease obtained from sheep's wool.

Cosmetics were used in Egypt as far back as 7,000 years ago. Today, millions of dollars are spent every year for such materials.

CRIME DETECTION: Every scientist is a sort of detective because he is constantly trying to find out Nature's secrets. But the chemist also helps police detectives in their work of tracking down criminals. A scrap of cloth, a flake of paint or a single hair found at the scene of a crime is often enough to show the chemist how the crime was done, or who the guilty person was. In Washington, the F.B.I. has large well-equipped chemical laboratories where all kinds of materials can be analyzed and identified.

INSECTICIDES: These are chemicals used for killing harmful insects that destroy valuable crops and household goods, or carry disease. One of the best of the newer insect killers was first prepared by United States government chemists during World War II. When you find out that the chemical name of this compound is *dichloro diphenyl trichloroethane*, you see why its name

has been shortened to DDT. When a solution of DDT is sprayed in the air, a thin coating of crystals of this compound is left wherever the spray settles. These crystals will continue to kill certain insects for months afterward.

There are dozens of other valuable insecticides. Some can be dusted or sprayed onto crops, while others are able to kill insect pests by gassing them.

WOOD PRODUCTS: In addition to its use in construction in the form of lumber, plywood and masonite, wood can be turned into cellulose for making plastics. Alcohol, acids, glue, and even sugar can be made chemically from wood.

One of our most useful wood products is paper. The wood—usually spruce, poplar or pine—is first changed to pulp by grinding. For the better grades of paper, chemicals are used to remove unwanted materials, leaving nearly pure cellulose. The pulp is bleached and mixed with clay or starch, and the fibers are matted together to form a thin sheet. This is run between heated rollers to give the paper a smooth surface.

PHOTOGRAPHY: Every step in making a photograph depends on chemistry. When you snap a picture, light from the scene you are photographing comes in through the camera lens and strikes the film. This causes a chemical change in the silver compounds that coat the film. It is then developed in a chemical solution, forming a *negative* of the scene. By shining light through the negative onto a piece of coated paper and then developing the paper, a *positive* print of the picture is finally made.

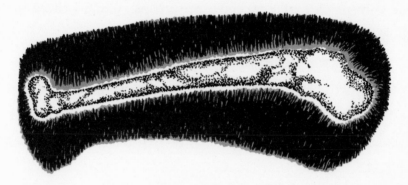

This bone was photographed by the glow of active atoms inside.

The chemical processes used in color photography are more complicated and make use of dyes to give the picture natural color.

ATOMIC ENERGY: This should really be called *nuclear* energy because it deals with the nucleus, or central core, of the atom and so this subject belongs to physics rather than chemistry. However, chemists do the important work of separating and purifying some of the materials needed in building "nuclear furnaces" (reactors), which we will soon be using as power plants.

The active materials that can be formed inside a nuclear reactor are helping chemists in their work. By building some active atoms into a compound, chemists can find out more about the way the molecules are put together. Biochemists feed activated chemicals to plants or animals in order to trace how foods are taken up by living organisms.

# 14.

# Your Place in Chemistry

In reading about chemistry and what it has accomplished you may have asked yourself, "Could I make chemistry my life work?" It is certainly a possibility worth thinking about.

In the United States, more than 150,000 people now work in the chemical profession and the number is growing all the time. Chemists are needed in factories, universities, museums, research institutes, hospitals, government laboratories, testing laboratories, and many other places. There are different kinds of jobs in these places, each requiring a certain kind and amount of training.

First, there are the *research chemists* who spend their time experimenting and forming theories that will add to what we know about chemistry. These people have studied chemistry in college and have usually gone on to do further work to earn the doctor's degree in science. Some research chemists work in colleges and universities, dividing their time between research and teaching.

A chemist with advanced training may decide to work for an industrial plant where he develops and improves some of the products you have read about in this book. He may call himself a *development chemist*, or a *chemical engineer*.

After research chemists have discovered the principles and development chemists have worked out ways of making things, there is still much to be done by others who understand chemistry. *Sales engineers* visit other factories to show the management how new chemical products should be used. *Technical writers* who know chemistry prepare instruction booklets, reports and descriptions of new products. These people probably studied chemistry in college, or may have learned the subject while working in a chemical plant or laboratory.

**A chemical librarian must know the language of chemistry.**

Wherever chemical work is going on there must also be people to help out professional chemists by acting as *laboratory assistants* or *technicians*. They may have gone into chemistry right after graduating from high school. Some may have taken special courses for the work.

Women as well as men can find interesting careers in chemistry. About one chemist in every twenty is a woman, and there are some chemical jobs where women outnumber men. A girl who knows something about chemistry in addition to office work can become a chemical secretary, and one who has studied library work and also is familiar with the language of chemistry can be-

**A research chemist spends much of his time experimenting.**

come a chemical librarian in a university or industrial plant.

How can you tell if *you* would do well working in chemistry? First of all, you need not be a "super-brain" to make good in a scientific field. The main thing is to have a real interest in the subject. Then you will develop the abilities that a scientific worker needs as you go along. If you like to read about new discoveries, if you enjoy tinkering and experimenting, if scientific subjects interest you—then you might think seriously about a career in chemistry.

There are some things you can do now. Read books

and magazines to find out all you can about chemists and their work, and arrange to visit nearby chemical plants. If some of your friends are also interested in chemistry, organize a Chemical Club. There are books that show how to do very interesting experiments using materials you can find around the house.

Then you will have a fair start in case you should decide to enter the wonderful world of chemistry.

# Index

# Index

# Index

allabout
books

EVERLY'S LIBRARY